Contagious
LEADERSHIP

10 STEPS TO TRANSITION FROM MANAGER TO LEADER

Monica L. Wofford

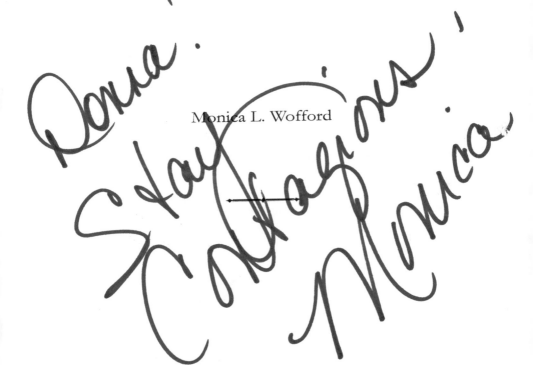

Donna · Stay Contagious! Monica

Contagious
LEADERSHIP

Monica L. Wofford

Published by:

Contagious COMPANIES™

Post Office Box 683316
Orlando, FL 32868
www.ContagiousCompanies.com
Info@ContagiousCompanies.com

Unattributed quotations are by Monica L. Wofford, CSP
Copyright ©2002, by Monica L. Wofford, CSP
2nd Edition Copyright © 2012, by Monica L. Wofford, CSP
15th Anniversary Edition Copyright © 2018, by Monica L. Wofford, CSP

Printed in the United States of America

Library of Congress Cataloging-in-Publication Data
Wofford, Monica L.
Contagious Leadership: Learning The Art of Successful Leadership
-1st edition
Includes biographical references and index.
W765.3.P04.2002
071.4'36'4207

"Experience is what you gain
from your own actions,

Wisdom is what you gain
from the experience of others..."

AUTHOR UNKNOWN

*shared with me by Nat Wofford,
my Dad, and source of wisdom*

May you be filled with wisdom...

TABLE OF CONTENTS

INTRODUCTION

Fifteen years!? Wow. And yes, you read that right. Fifteen years have happened since Contagious Leadership was first written. We could wax nostalgic about how time passes and how quickly it goes, or we could look at those things that have changed in leadership in those ten plus five years ago. The latter would be a short examination as the reality is that in real leadership, not much has changed. The environment in which we lead, however, has seen some alterations. We have new generations with their own set of challenges, which I've addressed in this new edition. We have far greater acceptance and awareness of emotional intelligence, which I've also sought to share this time around. We have issues of gender, personal choices, and mass eruptions of violent emotions that never seemed to pervade our landscape and leadership as they do now. We have both maverick and gracious, and deviant and determined examples of senior, national, and world leaders, though neither pair of qualities appear in the same person, which depending on who one models, could be a problem. What we don't have is a change in the fundamental concept. Leadership is still contagious. Good behavior and bad. In fact, everything you do, see, say, think, believe and how you behave, as a leader, rubs off on those you lead. Leadership is still about those you lead. If one believes otherwise, he or she is likely in a poor fit or possibly wrong, position. Leadership is still most frequently learned through mistakes, or trial and error, which is ironically exactly how the book you hold in your hand, came into being.

Have you ever made a mistake? I mean a huge, sloppy, red-in-the face kind of blunder? No, you say? CONGRATULATIONS! You are to be commended and you're most likely fibbing in spite of your actual knowledge to the contrary. Not to worry, I think I've made enough, and admitted most of them, for both of us. Mistakes are powerful learning mechanisms and many organizations, non-profits, and corporations still use them as the primary method for developing leaders.

Whether you, those you lead, those you want to lead soon, or those who lead you, have been given some magnanimous title as their claim to leadership fame simply volunteered when no one else would take the position, they're often left to figure out how to lead and the difference between management and leadership, on their own. This does not work in your favor, particularly if it's your boss we're discussing. They've been promoted, but not prepared. Don't be guilty of doing the same. Instead, follow the steps of Contagious Leadership.

This 15th anniversary edition will still help you learn the difference between management and leadership and when to use both, one, or neither. It still shines a light on the difference between authority, power, and leadership. And since it's original writing, a mere eight years following the dawn of the internet, a plethora of webinars, training classes, and keynote speeches have been developed and delivered that go deeper into each of those topics and the following ten steps, that form each chapter.

Contagious Leadership will help you define, discover, and earn respect. This book will guide you through finding value in each of those team members who look to you for leadership, even if it requires you employ a microscope. It will help you locate the internal kernel of potential in promotable people and it will impart wisdom and step by step instruction on how to build rapport, uncover value, ask for help and convey forgiveness.

You see, it's not just the leaders who blunder, but also those we call team members. Chapter 1 begins to address what Gen X and Baby Boomers still call them. Yet, when employees make mistakes, it's one of the greatest methods for learning. The leader who crucifies them for doing so, is actually slowing down the process and may be inadvertently ignoring the realities of what each generation values, as discussed in subsequent chapters. Or maybe, the leader suffers from insecurity and can't handle the impression an employee error will have on her or him. For this Chapter 3 comes to the rescue with guidance. Chapter 6 shows leaders the difference different methods of praise can make and Chapters 9,7,8 address the various facets of how a leader who is effective, communicates, which often resembles the order in which those chapter numbers are listed, out of order, the reason for which is a bit of a head scratcher.

For any leader who has been, in fact, promoted, but not prepared, if you desire to modify your current management style into one of leadership, or even increase the performance of those employees who report to you, this book will point you on the path of least resistance. The path, that is, that will allow you to get more out of those direct reports without need for a carrot or stick. If you seek detail on the logistics of specific HR issues, or employee discipline, please refer to any number of other talented authors who have come before me, and will continue to come after me. Particularly in the era of prolific lawsuits and entitled employees, there are many well-written books on these topics. If you seek help in dealing with difficult people and more on emotional intelligence, read Make Difficult People Disappear. It may also behoove you to know that if your beliefs, publicly, or privately, employ the words "my way is the only way" or if your personal motto is "my way is always the best", or if you believe secretly that the "good ole boy system" really is still the best way to do business, then the thoughts in this book may be a complete system shock. Worse yet, you may find that you cannot allow yourself to be open minded enough at this stage of your life to take in all the wisdom in these pages. (You would be surprised at what resistance I have seen to learning new concepts). Please do come back when you believe you are ready, or at the very least please take in only low doses of activity and rest while you read this book. And though you may think I am kidding, please know that much of what is said in the following pages is common sense to some, absolute modern dogma to others, a radical paradigm shift to still more, and a minor behavior modification to a large number of current and future managers. My low dosage warning is simply a humorous way to say that if you are shocked by what I say, take it slow and adopt what you can. One step at a time.

Contagious Leadership and it's robust and informative ten chapters were written to entertain, so that their ability to enrich, inform, and enlighten you is made easier. As a bonus, you will learn how to become a better leader, even if you are only paid to manage, even if you don't have a clue what the difference is between managing and leading, and even if you don't really feel like you need to know the difference or that it matters. The employees you manage wish you did, and know it does, even if you don't. In these chapters are the many mistakes I eluded to having learned earlier…and what I learned from them, that you now have the power to implement without the pain of learning the lesson in the way that seems hardest.

Leadership has great rewards, but also great struggles. It is not easy. Management, though easier to describe is far more transactional, less touchy feeling or needing to pay attention to the differences and needs in people. Leadership is all about the people you are leading, whereas management tends to be all about the one doing the managing and the tasks or steps. So, if this is all new or about to be new to you, you may find some of the stories and lessons ridiculously simple and exclaim "I would never do that!" Ever eaten those words before? You may also find yourself trying to apply the thoughts and practices in these chapters to real life. Oh NO! Real life cannot be like work! Real employees cannot be like real people with lives and families and values and dreams?! (Even those that have nothing to do with the job or career or office they currently participate in.) Do they not all check their humanness at the time clock or break room? No, they bring their humanness with them and it your job, my dear friend, to be the leader they need and to lead them. Remember, whatever you do in this endeavor to lead better will rub off on others. May your contagious efforts and actions be effective, positive, and long lasting!

Perhaps we should start at the beginning....

1 LEADERS VALUE AND RESPECT

Management *is* a privilege, though it may not always feel like it. So is leadership, but in most organizations, the privilege of leading comes from being promoted to a position with a management title and it's often the title that messes with people. Where most new managers fail is in focusing on their position instead of the people they have the privilege of leading. That mistake can lead to a complete loss of respect. That loss of respect can lead to negative behaviors, damage control and a bad reputation. Whoa! Let's back up a moment and start at the beginning. Even if you've been promoted, but not prepared, no matter how new or experienced you believe you are in leading others, you can build a strong foundation of leadership skills and prevent *all* of those things from happening. It starts with the knowledge that true leaders value and respect those they have the privilege of leading.

You may ask yourself, what difference does it make? Being a manager is an opportunity to have a captive audience paid to listen to you and potentially follow your directions. That captive audience is not, however, some version of Gru's Minions from Despicable Me movies, who live in the basement and eagerly await your directions. Nor are they a part of the Star Trek Borg population living in a cube and acting as one unit. They are not waiting eagerly to be "assimilated into your collective". The team, unit, department, or group you may manage, is made up of unique people with lives they lived before you became their manager and lives they will continue to live when you are no longer around. However, the impact you can have if you focus on being a leader, instead of just their manager, may stay with them far longer than you can imagine. This is one key fundamental difference between manager and leader. Do you want to be just a boss, or do you want to be a person remembered for having had a positive influence and impact on people?

> **Your impact as a leader stays with them far longer, and influences them far more, than you might currently imagine could happen.**

Employees are People

Impersonal words such as "direct reports," "subordinates," "underlings," or "my employees" are often used in place of "people." No. They are people, period. No more, no less. Yes, these words make describing the structure in which you operate far easier, but it is important to remember, particularly as you seek to become a better leader, that you are leading people. In some places they're called "units of productivity." In others, the attitude is that "Employees are liabilities." I was told, at age 19, by a second level manager, that employees were a "nuisance" and a "constant hassle." She, of course, must have been referring to all of my colleagues, versus me personally, so I was able to dismiss her flawed perception. The same way teenagers dismiss the lyrics in music, right? In truth, the power of her negative words stuck with me for several years and changed how I viewed those I had the privilege of working with from that point forward.

Thankfully that negative type of workforce climate has now largely changed. It is rare to hear a manager refer to team members in a denigrating manner and if he or she does, he or she visits Human Resources one or two times and is then on the hunt for a new position in a new organization. Yet, you will still hear "My people" and you do still hear references and labels that are negative and limiting. Efforts to mitigate the damage form those has prompted all kinds of inclusivity and diversity initiatives. Efforts to reduce the stress from these and other poorly placed labels, has led to incredible popularity of the book *Make Difficult People Disappear*. with so many accusing employees or millennials of being the difficult ones. Employees of diverse backgrounds are still people. Employees of differing generations, gender identification, race, creed, culture, language, personality, and religious preferences are still people. People, more than anything else we might call them, are complex. Leaders maintain the mindset that when leading, the differences in people must be considered, then accepted, then worked into the way in which one leads each team member.

We've come a long way from the days of discounting people's value publicly in the workplace and we've progressed past the days of being able to flagrantly deny value through lack of employment or promotion, in most cases. That pendulum has swung wide in that companies used to be able to choose the race or gender they worked with and are now mandated to fairly examine all employment choices, but it has also swung to the other side of feeling compelled to make hiring decisions based on elements other than skills or job-related criteria. Perhaps starting at the beginning means we keep this simple and just look at, well... people.

People have value. People, regardless of their values or background, are who you work *with* and they deserve respect. They deserve, and you benefit from, further examination beyond the surface. The whole team benefits from understanding each other, instead of using labels that are more damaging than accurately descriptive. Okay, simple. Managers work with people. But what does that mean, as a manager, you do with them? Somedays you manage their tasks, time off, and input. Other days you lead them. But, that leads to more questions. What does it mean to manage? Can you really manage people? And what does it mean to be a leader? Let's start there and build from those concepts.

A quick look at a web-based dictionary will show this for manager:

> **Manager** *n.* a person who manages; esp.,
>
> a) one who manages a business, institution, etc.
>
> b) one who manages affairs or expenditures, as of a household, a client (as an entertainer or athlete),
>
> c) an athletic team, etc.
>
> d) Baseball the person in overall charge of a team and the strategy in games
>
> e) in a school or college, a student in charge of the equipment and records of a team under the supervision of a coach.

A manager[1] is a person who manages and what that person manages is clearly defined as tangible elements, records, strategies and other inanimate objects. Yet, in last fifty years or more, we have learned to think of a manager as one who controls, directs, and leads people. Managers in fact, do not manage people. They manage peoples' actions, activities, and performance measurement. Leaders, however, lead unique people to use whatever unique gifts, skills, or talents each person has been given to perform the role he or she has been given. The act of leadership includes motivation, inspiration, development, recognition, delegation and many other widely discussed activities. As a culture, we've been told that looking at seats on the bus and putting the right people in them is leadership, when managing seat assignments is actually more about management. Managers have people reporting to them because of hierarchical structure; leaders have people following them, because of follower preference.

> **As a culture, we've been told that looking at seats on the bus and putting the right people in them is leadership, when managing seat assignments is instead, management.**

These differences are powerful. Treat the people who report to you, and whom you want to have follow you, as unique, and you will begin to behave like a leader. Files, records, and strategies do not care if you treat them as unique; people do, particularly those in the younger generations. In fact, millennials are far less entitled and difficult than imagined. They are in many cases, merely much more clear on their own value, confidence, and potential contribution to an organization.

With our backdrop of managers manage things and leaders lead people, we can make progress. Confuse those concepts and you end up with a conflict, or worse, disrespect, high turnover, and insubordinate team members. Acknowledge each employee as a person and show respect for the individual's value. This type of behavior for a leader is not limited to a span of control or hierarchy. Everyone is unique, so leaders treat everyone uniquely…and that, is not always easy. Your transition from manager to leader, and the shift leadership requires of a management mindset, begins here.

Stephen Covey may have been one of the first to succinctly clarify the manager versus leader difference is his book *The 7 Habits of Highly Effective People*. He said "Management is doing things right; leadership is doing the right things. Management is efficiency in climbing the ladder of success; leadership determines whether the ladder is leaning against the right wall."[2] Treating people uniquely is one of the walls of leadership. Do you know which wall you're leaning your ladder on?

Simple Words for Complex Beings

Said simply, the most important word a leader must keep in mind is the "P" word: People. Yet, if you spend your time trying to manage people, that P word often is replaced with "Pain in the neck". There is no substitute or even exchange for this living asset of people. No robot will do it. No software or computer replaces the ability for people to reconcile gut instincts, illogical conclusions or creativity.

Successful sports teams are living proof of the importance of the real "P" word in management and leadership. An athletic coach can be the greatest motivator, organizer, strategist, and taskmaster in the field, but he or she is ultimately dependent on the talent, courage, and dedication of the people recruited for the team.[3] The unfortunate truth is that most managers, particularly those newly promoted, never realize the difference between the coach of a team and the manager of the activities or output of an office or workplace. They continue to believe that management is about managing or controlling or being the one in control of people. When was the last time you tried to control someone?

The words are simple; management should be about people, but the concept is illogical and far from simple. It sounds almost too simple, given the proliferation of the word manager in most titles that actually require real leadership, but words are often simple. People are not. Deadlines are simple; getting people to meet them is not. Projects and tasks are simple; inspiring quality work from employees, motivating them to do their personal best, is not. So how is it done? How do you meet deadlines and inspire work that is perhaps even more than you asked for? Can you imagine? It's simple: acknowledge, recognize, and respect the unique nature and value of each of the employees you've been given the privilege to lead, while having the title of their manager. See her uniqueness and treat her according to who she is, not simply what you expect her to do. See his value and respect his worth to the team, department, and organization. If it's any consolation, admitting that each person who reports to you is unique, in all of its simplicity, *is* easy. Recognizing that particular unique trait or quality might be a little more difficult. Implementing this recognition and respect, if you have not done it in the past, can be downright tricky. This is primarily because it involves risk, vulnerability, confidence, trust and a significant dose of emotional intelligence. More simple words. Right?

We've said more than once that people are complex and yet untold numbers of organizations utilize simple assessments to try to simplify the needs

7

of people. Since the widespread adoption of the concept of emotional intelligence as a need for leaders, back in the 80's, assessments have been used in an attempt to bring clarity to an area of complexity. Use caution with these tools. Avoid the temptation to give out assessments, get new labels for people, and then require team members to wear name tags or display their personality label as if humans are just one type at all times. Use tools that have not come under scrutiny or questioning, as has the Myers Briggs Type Indicator which tells people perceiving or judging (the P or J in a four-letter result) are natural to a personality. They are not, but instead, are behaviors that can be demonstrated by any and all types. Use tools that combine the best of the intent, which is to find out more about each team member, so you can help them develop and communicate with them better, with favorable result and application. Help employees learn how they are unique. Learn how to speak their unique language and meet their unique needs so they respond better to your leadership, and encourage all to practice actually *using* this new awareness of each other. One such tool that meets these criteria and encourages action and training is the CORE Multi-Dimensional Awareness Profile®. (www.ContagiousCompanies. com/Assessments)

Acknowledge Them

Once you recognize unique value and accept differences, and whether you hire people as those who report to you, or you inherit them as existing employees who have been there longer than you have, remember this bit of wisdom. You do not purchase the people, their bodies, their brains, or their values[4] with the paycheck the company provides. What you do instead is rent, with that paycheck, their behavior and skills. This may be phone-answering behavior, problem-solving skills, truck driving behavior, sales and marketing skills, or strategic vision skills at an executive level; but it is still just behavior and skills that you rent, not the person, you purchase.

This sounds so obvious and yet, think for a moment about the average manager mindset on motivation. Often said silently is this statement: "We pay you. Isn't that enough motivation?" Ummm, no, it isn't. The person you hire must have demonstrated a superior ability with these behaviors and skills or chances are you would not have hired him to do the job, but how you motivate them to do more or learn more, is about leadership. If you have inherited someone and are not sure of the value of this unique employee to the team you manage, or to the planet for that matter, (though I assure you nearly everyone has significant value), try this simple exercise: ask more questions.

Ask Questions

It is mighty hard to recognize value from the corner office or the top floor or the cube in the front row. Your assumptions and labels will cloud your vision. If you plan to become better at leadership while in your position of management, you have to get up out of your workspace and make some people connections, you have to come in from the field or from visiting clients, come out of your office, and visit with those you wish to lead. This is now made easier with the concept of open workspaces and the relaxation of fraternization policies, but still bears mentioning. One of the best ways to begin to acknowledge a person is to find something the two of you have in common[5]. Ask them questions about the job. Heck, here's an idea, ask them questions about themselves, their desires, or what they think they do best. Ask them what they *love* to do outside of the office. Begin to recognize the value that each person brings to the group and organization, by showing an interest in what that value is or might be, in reality. (Better yet, try to find out what it is before you hire them.)

As a training manager, I frequently conducted interviews for training professionals. I used a three-phased interview that consisted of a telephone screening, a stand-up presentation, and a final question and answer session. During the telephone screening I asked questions about skills, past experience, and résumé-oriented information. During the standup presentation, a fifteen-minute prepared demonstration of training on a subject of their choice, I asked questions about classroom scenarios and curriculum content. If an applicant made it to the stand-up presentation, I had determined that he or she could at least articulate examples of the skills believed to be honed. The "stand-up," as I called it, was the applicants' chance to show those skills. During each stand-up presentation, other trainers and managers were invited to watch the presentation, after which they asked pre-planned questions that began with general knowledge and became gradually more specific. Some of the initial questions were, "If you had to have a project completed on a tight deadline, how would you go about rallying your resources and making it happen? Give me an example." Specific questions included "Tell me what your professional goals are over the next year." Or, "What have you done in the last six months to improve a weakness that you have?"

The entire process allowed me to ask questions and gain information needed in order to recognize the value of each individual and, make a connection. By the time I made a hiring decision I was pretty clear about what motivated and excited this person, and thus, about what I needed to do to maintain his or her sense of being a valued and unique member of the team. There are dozens of questions you could ask, but asking questions is just the beginning. What is more important is paying attention to the answers. Ask, and then truly listen.

If you inherit folks that have been around longer than dirt, often called veteran or senior or tenured employees, you may have to use a less structured, one-on-one interview process or more casual water-fountain, golf-course type conversations, when asking questions. Act like you're on Facebook having a chat with a new friend, in which you're interested in learning more about them. Harvey Mackay, a master salesman, author, and leader both at Mackay Envelope Company and in his seminars, developed a questionnaire specifically for this purpose. It allows employers to have a firm understanding of an employee through a series of thirty-three questions. The questionnaire, which appeared first in his bestseller *Beware of the Naked Man who Offers you his Shirt,* is an effective template to follow when looking for more questions to ask. Whichever questions you use to make the connection and uncover more information, I implore you to do two things:

1. Determine your questions and document them.

2. Guard and protect the information you get as if it were a precious treasure.

If making a connection with an employee is a new skill for you, a set group of questions will keep you from saying something unplanned or inappropriate, in a silent moment, to fill the space. These remarks often come out all wrong. And remember that the information you receive must be kept confidential unless they tell you, or you discuss this issue, otherwise. Personnel data can be very touchy and should be guarded carefully, even when what they love seems like something completely share worthy.[6]

Keep an open mind when seeking to acknowledge individual uniqueness, as the answer to your questions may provide a different perspective from what the outgoing manager told you or what you had already pre-judged in your mind. We do tend to let into the consciousness only those pieces of information which align with our already formed beliefs about others, the world, and ourselves. If your belief is that no one can be as good as you in a particular area, then you will tend to see only those responses which reinforce that idea. If you believe, based on word of mouth, previous experience, or other belief-building mechanism, that the person who now reports to you has no unique talent or skill in the area of his or her responsibility, then, true or not, what you will most readily see are behaviors and actions that reinforce your belief, unless you are able to keep an open mind. Though you may sometimes feel you need a microscope to locate it, there is value in each person. Let me repeat myself: *There is value in each person.*

I once had to focus on the color of a woman's gum for the first few minutes of an interview. It was an unusual blue and sort of glowed and was the only thing, at that moment, that interested me about the woman. She did not look the part of the person I had imagined would fill that job; she had arrived late to the interview; and I had been conducting interviews back to back since the early morning. I didn't want to appear as if my mind had already been made up before she even shook my hand, so I forced myself to stay open and give her the time that she deserved, simply by having shown up to the interview in question. She demonstrated admirable skills, a positive attitude and a dedication to her family of two children and two elderly, in poor health, parents. (She was only twenty.) I have always believed that if a person has the right attitude, a leader can teach the necessary skills. Staying open- minded and finding value in this, as it turned out, remarkable young lady, was a decision that I never forgot. She worked with me for the next three and-a-half years and won several awards as a top performer, even taking over as store manager long after I had left the company. Look carefully; the reality just may be different from what you originally thought. Managers only peruse the book cover and make a decision to purchase or not purchase. Leaders look for the back story, open the cover, and skim a few chapters before deciding.

Recognize Their Value

In the late 80s a good friend of mine shared one of her favorite books with me. (She thought that, as a new manager, I needed it, and I suppose

I should have taken the hint then, but some of us are more stubborn than others. Can you relate?) While written in a time that may feel no longer relevant, the book, *Coaching for Improved Work Performance*, by Ferdinand Fournies, first written first in 1978, made some pretty bold statements about the value of individual employees and their unique traits. This is now not a new concept and known widely intellectually. Yet, what we know or hear intellectually does not always show up in our actions. A book from the 70s or 80s has no less value than the shiny new article on LinkedIn. In fact, the frequency with which certain information shows up over time for us, may simply mean the indications that we actually need to learn or implement that lesson are increasing in intensity.

> **Policies are many,**
> **Good people are few.**
> **Policies will change.**
> **People rarely do.**

One statement from that book that has stuck with me for years is about personality traits and what a manager must know about each employee in order to recognize his or her value. Now, one obstacle that hinders both managers and leaders is the unending encouragement received from books and seminars to recognize each of their subordinates as being different. We are told we must treat them as individuals, according to their differences. This concept is fine if it stopped there. (Haven't I been saying much the same thing?) The trouble is, the theory is usually supported by detailed explanations of the personality quadrants or types or categories throughout the population. In many cases, these are merely more labels if one doesn't take the information further and explore subtle differences and how to actually use this information.

As a manager, you are often led to believe that knowledge of these categories and quadrants will equip you with the ability to identify individual personality differences and, therefore, to adapt management efforts to fit that mold. This seems logical in view of all the sources claiming knowledge and know-how about the complexities of man, but it left Ferdinand, and still leaves me, with one important question: "Do managers have to understand as much about people as psychologists do, to successfully manage them in business?"[7] Is this also true for leaders? Well, yes, and no.

Both seem like important questions because if the answer is yes, then the next question is even more startling: "How in the Sam Hill do you do that without a PhD in psychology?" Thus, I say NO, neither a manager nor a leader needs to be as skilled or as educated as a PhD in psychology to determine how to treat each person as unique and different, but both need to be aware of how these differences impact value, respect, and performance. There is a saying that describes what happens to those who gain a little knowledge and then proceed as if they are the experts. If you "know just enough to be dangerous," do not pretend to be the expert. This could be considered what we call practicing without a license, which may get you into serious trouble, or more likely, cause you to attempt to lead based on assumptions and one simple label. It may also keep you from achieving the real point: To get to know those who work with you and how they like to be treated.

A Word on Assessments

There is tremendous value found in the body of work known as Emotional Intelligence, or what is often called EQ. The greatest value is in learning how to USE the information and yet a plethora of organizations will employ a tool that just provides more labels. Before you compare the team you lead to dogs, animals, shapes or colors, consider the actual people you're putting through an assessment and the purpose for doing it in the first place. If the purpose is to learn how to work together even more effectively or even to reduce the presence of difficult miscommunications, then use a tool that addresses those areas specifically and is facilitated by actual humans. For those aspiring to become positively Contagious Leaders, the CORE Multi-Dimensional Awareness Profile® is recommended. Available online, this tool provides a report, three graphs, an online reference manual to use long after completion, and a coaching call for results validation. Assessments that only come with a report and no human facilitator to review or train on use of results, are likely to provide inaccurate data as 54% of the population does not know themselves well enough to accurately self-report. Also, until such time as you make the decision to provide a full assessment to each person, there is a short/quiz-like version of the profile, also online, that will get you started with the basic descriptions of differences.

www.ContagiousCompanies.com/CORESnapshot

15

There is a difference between what psychologists do and what managers and leaders benefit from doing. Managers, while directing activities or tasks, are simply faced with understanding the communication style that works best for the person to whom they are sharing directions, and the skills that are best suited to that person. Leaders, while motivating or often inspiring and developing, focus on these same traits, but take it one step further and look more closely at their own behavior and how it can dramatically affect the behavior of the employee and may need modification in a multitude of circumstances. You might say that managers use the Golden Rule. Do you remember what that was? It always makes me chuckle when I ask this question in a keynote or training session and three out of thirty people can actually recite the rule: Do unto others as you would have them do unto you. In case you are of those twenty-seven remaining participants, is it coming back to you now? If so, consider it, and then let us look at another option. Leaders would benefit more from something known as the Platinum Rule. The Platinum Rule, created by Dr. Tony Alessandra, author of Relationship Strategies[8], is:

Do unto others as they would want to be done unto.

What this means is simple: Recognize the value of each individual, understand their skills, and identify their unique way of communicating, and how that aligns with their expected contribution to your organization. Then treat them in a way that speaks to them, that they understand, as opposed to the way that speaks to you and with which you are most comfortable. Respect speaks to everyone but means something different to each person and is conveyed in different ways by each person. (Sometimes I think it is pure marvel that we understand each other at all.) Simply put, learn about the different personalities. Assess a person's label and then learn what that label means and what that means the person labeled needs from you, their leader. Then, and this is a big one, learn how to modify the actions you take to get what you need, which could differ immensely, in ways that meet and motivate that person based on their needs.

Respect: Find Out What It Means... To Them

When you respect people you work with, or even those you have not yet begun to work with, the results can be amazing. Communicating in another person's unique style or language or with acceptance of what they need that may be different, is a form of respect. One meeting I held in New Orleans with five tenured employees I had not yet met, to which I was thirty minutes late, could have been a disaster, had I not been able to communicate differently with each person. It is best to communicate in a style that suits the person to whom you're talking. This does *not* mean mocking or copying the person in front of you. It simply means picking up on their use of vocabulary, speed, comfort level with topic, and many other details that we will delve into with more fervor later. Remember Tony Alessandra's *Platinum Rule*.

On the occasion in New Orleans, I had been asked by my boss to call the meeting (on very short notice) for the purpose of telling these employees that the current location of their work was changing. I had been promoted to be their manager only weeks prior to this meeting. This meant that if they wished to remain in that job, moving would be required. If they didn't want to move, they would need to find a new job. Surely, there was better material for dinner conversation and a first meeting. What I am told made this news easier to swallow, for each of them, was that I positioned myself in front of each person, right there, at and around the table. I mirrored the first team member's body language, matched his facial expressions and spoke to him in the communication style that I had observed him using in the first fifteen minutes of small talk while we ordered dinner.

One of the nicest compliments I ever received was from this gentleman, the only man at this table and on this team, who pointed out something that I had not realized at the time, I'd been doing. Upon leaving the restaurant, this man, who now had to move to another city and state or continue the same work, thanks to my message, stopped me and said:

> *"I am just amazed at how you delivered that news to each of us in just the right way, so we could handle it, and you did it differently for everyone. It made it so much easier to hear when you said it in a way that was comfortable for each of us. I mean, you talked to Cindy in her own way, Melissa in a more direct, serious way, and..."*

It took some time for me to realize how I had incorporated this style. I had not done it on purpose at the time. What had happened was that I felt compassion and empathy for these people, and that was clearly coming out in my communication. I cared enough to learn more about who they were and what they needed. I cared about how they received this message and perceived me as their new manager. I wanted them to be at least comfortable with the person they heard it from and the way it was delivered. You see, when you are comfortable with the person you are speaking to, you tend to mirror his or her body language quite naturally. It is a simple function of human communication. In this case it allowed me to show respect by doing unto others as they wanted to be done unto. It also improved my ability to communicate clearly and be understood. In Chapter 7, I have broken down the specific communication steps that occurred. And here's something I learned: In this case, and in many others since, communicating the message was not nearly as difficult as communicating the respect—and it's the respect that makes the difference.

New communication skills take some time and practice, but the payoff is enormous. If you can deliver tough news in a communication style that is more suited to the individual, conveys respect and individual value, and thus has a less painful reaction, you're practicing leadership. Managers focus on the message. Leaders focus on the recipients. Ever had to let go of an employee you valued, due to budget cutbacks? The respect then may have been easier because of sincere empathy for that situation. Ever had to let go of an employee you were glad to see go? The respect in the latter may have come less naturally. Nevertheless, was just as important.

Once you have defined your role or become comfortable and clear with what you are expected to do and are expected to manage or lead (as you must be clear before you begin to clarify it for others), then take the next step. Acknowledge the people who report to you and their individual value. Ask them questions about their skills, gifts, talents, abilities, and weaknesses. Once you recognize that they have value, in what areas that value resides, and how it can best be utilized in the position they currently hold, your ability to show respect to them will grow.

3 Steps to Respect Uniqueness

- Acknowledge and accept each person as an individual

- Recognize his or her value to you, the team you manage, or the organization.

  - Show each person respect in a way that is clearly understood by that person.

The better you get at recognizing, not only that the people you wish to lead are unique, but also the ways in which they are unique, the closer you will come to delivering your message clearly and effectively, being understood more readily. After all, that is the whole point, is it not?

If you come by these skills naturally, be aware that there are many managers, wishing to become leaders, who must practice this skill of recognizing uniqueness and who did not arrive on the planet with such a broad appreciation for everyone. Be patient, and glad that you already have it mastered, and then add it to your tools needed for leadership and work to improve the gift you've been given.

Pardon, Whom Do You Work for Again?

If you can stomach the idea that each employee is unique and has individual value, then you may also subscribe eagerly to the belief that each manager is unique. Even in their uniqueness, however, many managers seem to share a common belief about employees. That belief is that employee's work FOR managers, as well as working FOR the company that pays both of your paychecks. You have heard the phrases "I work for so and so," or "She works for me over in accounting." No? If this nonsense is common conversation for you and your workplace colleagues, allow me the privilege of asking you to recognize that people don't work FOR you, or a company, or a business. People work for money, fulfillment, obligations, children or elderly in their care, a mortgage, car payments, kids in college, pets, and a whole host of other reasons. Would you believe some people even work for the prevention of boredom, the achievement of a dream, or the enrichment of their life through their achievements at work? Some people actually work to get *away* from that beloved family and children!

Whether said in jest or with even a grain of sincerity, the phrases "You work for me" and "My employees" and "I work for XYZ Company" are very simply not true and a bit dated. Yes, these people are employed by and often receive a paycheck from you or the company or entity you represent. It makes no difference if you are a corporate CEO with 500 direct employees or an entrepreneur with one employee. Neither the 500 nor the one, works FOR either company. So, what exactly is the difference between being paid or employed by and working for an entity? Let us view this thought from a different angle. Employees do not, in most cases, complete work, meet deadlines, stay late, work overtime, go the extra mile for the customer, or help you with a last-minute crisis, for the purpose of making your day, as the manager, or your Boss's Day, or for spending those extra few moments of quality time with you, no matter how nice a person you are or how much fun you are to hang out with. Refer back to the list of reasons, a few paragraphs back, of why people work and whom they are actually working FOR.

If you still believe these people work FOR you, try telling those same employees that you can still employ them in their current position, but it will be without pay. If they agree to the arrangement (and you are not employing volunteers for a charitable organization), then you will have proven me wrong. More importantly, you will have proven these people are following a leader they believe in regardless of their compensation. Were this experiment put into action, however, in a corporate or for-profit environment, I believe the results would be immediately clear in most organizations. It is not FOR you that employees work, nor is it always for money, but rather for what that money can provide or for the fulfilment the role or cause they support, provides. In truth, none of us works for anyone other than ourselves, and thus we all work *with* each other. The sooner you are able to recognize this, verbalize this, and begin to work *with* the employees that you manage, the sooner they will work *with* you and follow your lead.

All right, then, how do you implement this new style of behavior and thought? First comes a critical piece of recognizing uniqueness: determine what each employee you are working with, is working for, and realize it is likely not for the privilege of seeing you or your manager's smiling face daily. Start small with the following exercise. First, imagine yourself as a new employee in what you consider a "dream job." You are hoping to make a good impression on your boss and his boss in your first staff meeting. You have spent an extra twenty minutes on your hair or beard, or face, worn your favorite suit, and have just arrived at your new office. Your new boss and his senior manager immediately greet you. After formal introductions, the senior manager begins to converse with your boss about plans for his team. Your boss says, "I have great plans for my team. In fact, [your name] is going to do a great job for me, aren't you?" If this were your real situation, this would be the real moment of truth! Who are you working for? And do you appreciate being talked to like a puppy? It seems innocent enough, and so many people do it, so it seems normal, right? In your scenario, the conversation continues as the senior manager asks your boss for results of his team. Your boss tells him, "My team is doing well, and my employees are working really hard to achieve the quotas you set. My highest producer is beating his own record and my three new hires are coming along nicely." If this imaginary boss of yours realized these were individuals he was describing, it seems odd that his word choice could just as easily have been applied to animals or stick figures. If this were you as the manager, how would you do it differently? Or *would* you do it differently?

Once you have gone through imagining your scenario, as vividly as possible, determine if it feels natural or uncomfortable. If it feels natural, then you may be subconsciously treating those people who report to you like cute little minions, condescended to like children, who should follow you around and heed your command, as if you saved them from disastrous consequences by letting them work for you and your magnanimous management. Detect that sarcasm. The analogy may seem harsh, but people form strong perceptions when given condescending treatment, and the above scenario can be seen as very condescending. If you began to treat people differently by simply saying that they work WITH you, people notice, and so will you. Work hard to monitor your language choice, and that will change the way you think about those who have been assigned to report to you. If you have imagined this scenario, and it seems very unlikely that you would treat someone in that manner or say those things, then you may not be exhibiting traits that tell people you believe they work FOR you, or at least not explicitly. To keep yourself in check or monitor exactly what you do say that could be construed as condescending and less than respectful, ask one or two trusted people you work with to listen for specific phrases and words that might resemble "my team," "my employee," "my people," "they work for me" and other such expressions. You may find that you do not use such vocabulary, or you may find that simply raising your awareness will eliminate this minor issue from your management practice and take you further toward exhibiting real leadership.

It Really is All in How You Say It

The use of different words, though it may seem a silly matter of semantics, can make a big difference. A noticeable change occurs when a manager begins to describe employees as those she works WITH instead of those who work FOR her. If the manager in the previous example had said "The team is doing well, and we are working really hard to achieve the quotas you set," the message would have been different. The subtle, seemingly simple, change is powerful and effective, and tends to unite team members, instead of inciting internal conflict or sabotage efforts. Remember, early on I told you some of these lessons may seem very obvious and simple? Your next exercise is to take one day to list all the times you mention the people on your team, or in your office, who are supervised by you as "your employees" or as "work/working for me." All is not lost, if even with the help of others and after a day of monitoring you feel you cannot break the habit of saying, "my team" or "those that work for me," or if you find nothing wrong with the scenario with the new boss. For some companies this is an acceptable part of corporate culture, and the bosses feel it is never used to imply a condescending hierarchy. However, I believe if anyone asked the opinion of the employees described this way, the employees would feel differently!

Once you become aware of the impact of what you are saying or what is being said to you, despite the intent of corporate cultures, you may start to make small efforts to change, if being a leader of people is truly what you want to attain. Use the approach of starting small to make that change and realize that the habit of speaking that way took a while to learn, and will take a while to un-learn.

In a conversation, if you say, "my employees," remind yourself that you could say it differently and try again next time. Instead, say, "the team I work with." Or try to include "the group that reports to me" or "the group that I work with." I have often said the team that "I have the privilege of managing." or the "team I have the privilege of leading". It is truly very effective to describe employees as those you "work with." and for whom you see your role as a privilege. It may confuse those around you at first, yet once explained will clearly send a message of your change in focus and perspective.

But, They Do It Different

You may find that other managers are uncomfortable with your change, as it points out the impact that they, too, are having, if they choose not to change. In fact, you may begin to get questions about why you are describing the team that reports to you in that manner. No problem. Many a great leader has made others uncomfortable by being different. Different is not a bad thing. Different is not the same as difficult. Each of us is unique, thus different, and allowed to behave in ways that work well with our own style. Unfortunately, many managers and high-powered individuals have also cut corners or made dangerous short cuts with assessments and assumptions about the concept of different. It is much faster to say, "my team" or "my employee" than to say, "the team I work with" or "the employee who reports to my organization." or the "team I have the privilege of leading". It is also much faster to build a mobile home than a brick home with a cement foundation. Which will stand the test of time and next hurricane sized change, as well as bring a greater value to your figurative estate? When it comes to other managers and their comments, reactions are often motivated by competition, envy, or misunderstanding, or even the "that's not the way we do it around here" mentality. Educate those who wish to know, even sharing this chapter with them, and let go of the others by politely removing yourself from the conversation.

To be sure, you must be aware that the team that reports to you talks with the team that reports to your colleagues. And they talk about everything, even what you do not tell them, even what you ask them not to share. People will know what you're doing. You may be in a position to educate your colleagues on communicating with and about the team they manage or possibly even lead, and the impact this "you work for

**Different is NOT
the same as difficult.**

me" type of language is having, if the topic arises. The point of such education is to increase the level of respect on the team your colleague manages, for his or her own good, so to speak, but also to cut down on the miscommunications and perceptions that so often turn into juicy gossip and painful rumors.

It is probably best not to approach colleagues with a potential lesson "they need to know." Rather, try saying there's something you would like to share with them. Share your book with them, thus avoiding the risk of offending someone who is merely doing what has been accepted in our country's corporate culture for years. Lead their potential change in perspective, rather than attempting to manage their choices in behavior.

Recently I was in a social setting with several people I work with, of all different levels. Of course, the conversation strayed to business, and one of my peers said, "My team and my trainers are very involved in that project.' I responded with nothing more than "So is the team I work with. They have been very busy with that project". She looked at me for half a second, smirked a little sideways, and began to copy my verbiage in her next sentence when she said, "You know, as busy as they have been, I am really proud of the work that the team that reports to me has accomplished." And, no, I hadn't harped on this lesson with her before; I had mentioned it and then left it alone, not wishing to force someone else to change behavior that she was perhaps not ready, nor comfortable, with changing. Leaders know that everyone comes to an idea at a different speed and that allowing them to learn at their pace is more effective than forcing the pace you may have chosen.

It could have just rubbed off as a result of my leading by example for an extended period of time. On the other hand, maybe she was making fun of me. Who knows? I do know those employees that report to her noticed and said to her later that they appreciated being publicly acknowledged and praised for their efforts. How did they know, you ask? Ever heard of the grapevine?

From the time we are children, we are told to be respectful of others. Many of us also heard "respect your elders" and if we did not hear it at home, we heard it on a myriad of sitcoms, or in the form of advice from wise on-lookers in our lives. Why respect is not an automatic response for all people, everywhere, is one big mystery for me. Yet, the fact remains: Respect is everyone's birthright. The opinion that I share with many who are reaching out for a return to civility and respect is this: Everyone on the planet deserves respect. Even those you find to be the most difficult to manage, much less lead.

The Kind and Gentle Lesson

YouTube and other social media channels are filled with videos of this lesson. Respect those who are homeless. Black lives matter. Small children can actually be respected for their large talents. We seem to grasp this concept or even be quite open to it, personally. Yet, at the office, it continues to remain another matter or at least lesson for which we need more reminders. I have seen many managers who were very respectful to those who were senior managers, often Vice Presidents or Directors, and yet treated the "elder" or fifty-six-year-old woman who reported to them as if she couldn't perform her job without their exclusive direction, expertise, and input. In fact, I confess: I've been that manager.

Respect would tell me to ask her what questions she has and to make sure she is confident she has all the tools necessary for job completion. Respect would tell me to ask for her input on many issues, as she may have solved my, and our, problems many times before this employment scenario. Respect would tell me to treat her much as Anne Hathaway's character treated Robert Deniro's, toward the *end* of the movie *The Intern,* instead of the discounting of value shown in scenes at the beginning. This includes much more than calling her ma'am or an older gentleman, sir.

What I should've realized as a twenty something manager with a fifty-six-year-old team member is that with her fifty-six years, came a unique perspective on the customers, the business, and the importance of the almighty dollar versus true customer service. Fortunately for my ego and my career, this fifty-six-year-old employee on the team I managed and worked with, had more grace and poise than I possessed at the time. She continued to let me learn on my own, from the mistakes I was making. Never once did she say, "I told you so." Never once did she say, "If you would just listen to me and do it my way, you would save yourself a lot of time."

I think secretly she enjoyed watching me make my mistakes (or learning experiences), but that may have been more maternal than malicious. In her heart, I think she knew I would disregard her advice and force myself to learn the hard way. I have always been good at that, as the difference between experience and wisdom has not always been clear, nor top of mind, much less, a reminder that one could seek the wisdom of others instead of gaining the experience personally. Both concepts have eluded me in my practice of business management in the past. (See quote in the front of the book if they still elude you, as well.)

Shortly after I left that position, as manager of a ladies' clothing retail store, I began to recognize my misjudgment and her uniqueness. I began to respect her gifts. I realized that I had been given the privilege of working with a part-time salesperson who was reliable, punctual, and present in her job, because she liked her customers, and they liked her. She did not work for me or for money, but for the ability to get out of her house, be with people, earn a little extra spending money and make a difference.

All of my expertise in retail and selling could not teach her those things. Carolyn, wherever you are now, bless your heart for letting me gain the experience, even though you had wisdom to share. From you, I learned that an individual's strength and experience is better recognized than ignored, and that those who work with me may know more than I, even though they may keep that a secret until their manager shows it safe to share that wisdom.

Apparently, I Still Had Not Learned the Lesson

A few years later, as manager for a different industry and several wireless retail stores, I worked with a staff of twelve people and a bevy of very special customers. In addition to hiring, firing, customer service, scheduling and the like, part of my unwritten responsibility was to answer business calls on the company-provided wireless phone, 24 hours a day, 7 days a week. Customers did not typically call at three a.m., so after business hours a call usually meant a burglary at one of the three locations for which I was responsible.

One of the stores (which I must point out was an inanimate object, with no feelings or real needs, unlike the people I worked with) was less than a mile from President George Bush Senior's residence in Houston, Texas. This was not a high crime area and the location was rarely burglarized. My home was a traffic-clogged fifteen or twenty miles from the store, which In the city of Houston, can mean thirty minutes, even at two o'clock in the morning. Several members of the team I worked with lived much closer to the store than I. During one chilly winter week, the alarm brought me to the store in my pajamas to determine the cause of its activation and apprehend the no-good burglar, or at least witness the police in action. The officer and I had a friendly conversation about mischievous kids in the area and the lack of broken glass or missing goods, prompted me to again drive all the way back home. The next call, again at two a.m., happened three days later. I took the call, and this time called a team member and asked that he drive to the store, less than two blocks from his home. I convinced myself that he would "gain development" from meeting the officer at the scene. At least that was my story.

Twenty minutes later, I received a call from him saying that there had been a real break-in, complete with shattered glass and stolen phones and accessories, and that the police were there actively investigating. I arrived twenty-five minutes later to begin my work and send the team member home, as he did not need to be involved in the inventory of what was left of the merchandise. This had always been deemed the manager's responsibility but offered the team member little opportunity for "development", particularly given the presence of a control freak of a manager who believed she had to do all her own inventories.

Much to my chagrin, his girlfriend had come with him to the store. Both looked emotionally drained and exhausted, and there was tension in the air as if I my call had interrupted one of those relationship types of conversations. I chose not to ask that night, but I later found out that they had been arguing most of the evening and into the morning about her terminally ill mother, and that he had begged her to come because he was afraid he would get in trouble if he did not obey my request to address the storm alarm in the dark of night. The fate of this couple's relationship certainly did not turn on my one request, but it taught me that one simple respectful question gains a lot of ground with employees, team members and people, in general. The question is, "Did I catch you at a bad time?"

At the slightest hint of hesitation in response to this question, when I called after hours, even at two in the morning, I would have apologized for the inconvenience and arranged to call them back at another time, or at least made the request with much more knowledge of the unintended consequences. My unwillingness to fulfill my responsibilities because of what felt like an inconvenience did not constitute a need to interrupt someone else's personal life, merely because of their geographic proximity to my problem. My crisis was truly just that, MY crisis. To give it to someone else shows disrespect and is just plain lazy. However, managers at times are guilty or there wouldn't be humor in the jokes that talk about managers pushing off all unpleasant tasks to team members

Real emergencies cannot be helped, and during work hours other arrangements can sometimes be made, but respect for the personal time of those whom you have the privilege of leading, and whose activities you manage, is crucial. Had I been respectful of this employee's unique situation, instead of managing by command through fear, he could have shared his predicament, we could have made a decision and ultimately, I would have been at the store sooner and could have gone back to bed an hour earlier, without feeling guilty over impacting the personal life of a team member. Hindsight is a beautiful thing! The lesson for me then, that has stuck with me for years since that incident, was to begin asking the question, "Did I catch you at a bad time?" and listening for the real answer, despite the response that may be conditioned. My bigger lesson was to learn not to call after hours at all! Much of that has now been mandated for organizations, but still has many organizational culture exceptions. Management is still a position somewhat expected to be on call 24/7, but with regulations in place that are more robust and generations who value quality of life over undo dedication to an office, the lessons are still relevant. Both lessons were needed and were different from what I learned from Carolyn, but each deal with respect and the value of others. I also continued to apply these principles to other areas. For example, I have found it imperative to respect the time when those you work with are away from the office on scheduled, appropriate lunches, or on vacation, and to strongly encourage that they use it without calling in to talk with you about work. You may find it preposterous that employees would actually be so committed to their work that they would call in while on vacation to discuss an idea or project they are working on at the time. Yet, in my personal experience, this is a byproduct of leadership: creating exceptionally dedicated future leaders who are passionate about what they do and want to share it with you, even when they are being paid not to think about work. That kind of drive is not something you can't buy, but it is often something you will get when you respect and value each person's unique skills, abilities, talents, and gifts.

Simply encouraging those you work with to take the time off will allow them the time for "re-creation", often disguised as recreation and time off. Both you and the employees benefit from this time away from work, but if they cannot leave you alone, then hear them out and explore the idea. Some of the world's best leaders have perfect solutions that pop into their brain at two in the morning, vacation or no vacation.

If you find that it is you who are unable to leave them alone, that you continue to call and ask "just one more question" or provide "just one small project that is a condition of their employment" while employees are on vacation, then I venture to say you are mis-managing and certainly mis-leading by putting all the eggs for that project or question in one basket, namely the one on vacation. Cease and desist calling employees who are on vacation, unless you wish them to feel compelled to track you down in your hotel room, while you are vacationing in Cancun, to go over a floor plan question. (True story!)

Refrain from training those who work with you that they cannot do it without you and you cannot do it without them. Unique individuals with value are pretty darn resourceful. Nothing will burn down when they are on vacation or on a day off, or when they leave at five. In our world of fast-moving business deals and changes, this may be hard to believe. However, there is something to consider if it does feel as if things are falling apart if one member of the team is absent. Is there an opportunity for cross-training? Perhaps you have over-delegated or not been involved enough. Perhaps it is time to re-evaluate the attention you pay, not only to each employee's uniqueness, but to each employee's growth. Did I just hear you say…

"But aren't they adults?"

"Aren't they responsible for their own growth?"

...work with me on this one.

2 LEADERS TAKE INTEREST IN GROWTH

Growth can be personal or professional, though growth from a mere manager's perspective is tied to numbers, or an increase in output. Leaders, however, view growth on a larger scale and look at the overall development of the person. But, some still say reality sounds like "Why should I care about the growth of my employee—uh—the people I have the privilege of managing? Isn't it enough that the company provides their paychecks and gives them time off?" Contagious Leaders take interest in the growth of those they have the privilege of leading, as well as their development and their potential.

Adding to the difference between manager and leader, there is a large gap between enough, or good enough, and great. Managing is good enough; leadership is great. Whichever you're doing now is enough. Start with where you are and what you know. Learn more about your employer's criteria and ensure you add that into the mix of your own development and behavior. Then, if you wish to transition to leadership or become a better leader, you also want to add a focus that shows at least an interest in the growth of these unique people you have the privilege of leading.

Being interested in a person's growth can take a number of forms, and it will usually gain you his or her respect. It could also result in an increase in their dedication, and often loyalty, if done with sincerity. More importantly, it will develop more productive, fulfilled and effective employees. If, in the past, you have displayed little or no interest in the employees on the team you currently manage and their needed growth, then start small and MEAN it. If you are not truly interested and have little or no desire to care yet believe a growth focus is part of your future promotion strategy, then we probably need to have a different conversation. That's like running for political office and saying you care about your voters, when in reality all you care about is getting elected to the next highest position. People, employees and voters, sniff out that lack of congruent behavior, in a hurry! Being sincere in your care or concern for each team member happens to be one more you show your respect and value for their unique needs and contributions, a nice side benefit if you're now building on your Chapter 1 efforts. Not caring about this area, or missing this next step in your leadership journey, will nearly always cause you to stumble or even fail as a leader, ensuring you remain an individual performer. They'll stop listening to your advice and stop heeding your direction because most adults, employees and people believe in some way that unless you are influenced by my uniqueness, I am not going to be influenced by your advice.

> ## Unless you are influenced by my uniqueness, I am not going to be Influenced by your advice.

Another mistake, fatal to your leadership endeavors, listed by Steven Brown, in his book *13 Fatal Errors Managers Make and How You Can Avoid Them*, is to FAIL TO DEVELOP PEOPLE. In fact, it is fatal mistake number two! Even more telling is that fatal mistake number ten is FAIL TO TRAIN YOUR PEOPLE. We won't fault Mr. Brown for calling these employees "your" people, as his book was written long ago, but it is important to note that training and developing those teams and the people you supervise is critical. If you do not care and you do not develop, you won't be leading for long, either.

Growth Can Be Many Things

Providing training for new knowledge and skills is one area of growth and one form of development. In large-sized offices, or a corporate setting, training is usually available to employees on a regular basis, sometimes even from internal sources or training departments. Some companies have created the equivalent of online universities and allow employees to train from their desk or engage in vendor provided webinars. Ensure that those who report to you have this made available to them whenever possible. Those with the greatest of initiative and a tendency toward continuous self-improvement are Google-ing solutions and training and information to meet their needs even without your encouragement. Partner with their existing efforts. Support their need to attend classes and let them take time away from current responsibilities. Why? Because the time away will allow for them to refresh their creative juices and their drive. Even those who are resistant to training you may send them to, whether the employee sees the training as a prison, a vacation or an excuse for a day off, especially if it is off-site or in a classroom format, will benefit from the change of pace from the daily routine. The change is what often sparks new ideas. Do keep in mind though that a one-day training class will not fix all the issues, no matter how good the class or the teacher.

Training does work for development and continued growth and improvement. Training even works and is an option on a tight budget and even with the most obstinate of characters. To make it more effective, you don't just send her on her merry way to a class with no guidance; you set expectations of the employee prior to her classroom experience. Ask her to look for two for three specific things, that don't require you to know the curriculum inside and out and let her know that you look forward to sitting down with her soon after the class to hear of her findings and what she liked most and learned from this training. It is as simple as that, but often reality looks more like this:

Manager: "How was your class?"

Employee: "Oh, it was fine. Thanks."

Manager: "Good. Got that report ready?"

Employee: (thinks) "I have been out of the office for the class you sent me to! How did you expect me to still get that done?

If you have ever talked with a child after he or she returned from school and asked, "What did you do in school today?" you've likely heard the familiar response of "Nothin'." The same happens with adults and training programs. In fact, it is no different with adult learning results, and the expectations you set prior to training can make all the difference.

How to Make the Most of Training as Development

- Clarify and set your expectations for their learning

- Share your expectations before the training

- Request the employee to look for 2-3 specific points, take-aways, or ways to apply the training content provided

  - Establish time to debrief after the training program

  - Keep that appointment

There is also a secondary benefit to setting aside a meeting with this employee after the training. Most people love to receive special attention, and if you make it known that each time someone leaves the office to attend a training course, he will get to spend thirty minutes with you and have exclusive use of your time, you will see an increase in the desire to attend training, and the desire to pay attention in said training. By the same token, if *you* believe training to be a waste of time, a vacation, or a prison, then do not act surprised when the people you manage, and wish to lead, behave as if they believe the same. Lead by example, not by masking what you really think. Most people see beyond the mask. Employees are not telepathic, but they can sniff out a phony pretty quick! Hmmmm…do we see a pattern in what commonly trips up new leaders and gets sniffed out by others?

Strengths AND Non-Talents

A wonderful book graced the shelves of many bookstores not too many years ago. *First Break All the Rules* became the guide for the way some business got done and leaders believed they were going to get results. With thousands of data points, Marcus Buckingham and Curt Coffman, of The Gallup Organization, put together a series of best practices that were provided by people whom the authors believed to be the best managers out there. They told readers that the best managers focused on strengths, essentially spending the most of their time with their best people or giving most of the attention and opportunities to the top performers. This work then became the basis for a program known as Strengths Finders, and several books that followed.

The logic in their process is solid. In fact, the first time I read *First Break All the Rules*, I even realized that I was spending inordinate amounts of time with those team members who needed the most guidance, and seemingly the most training, thus perpetuating the behavior that was gaining them attention. Coffman and Buckingham have succinctly and scientifically explained why this is so, but it all boils down to the human's basic need for attention and understanding.

The best managers know that humans crave attention. Each individual might value different kinds of attention, but for each person, we all dislike being ignored. (though yes, if that negative Ned in your office would ignore you for the next millennia, that would be okay, too) The challenge arises when someone we wish liked us, admired us, thought highly of us, or thought of us in any way positive at all, seems indifferent or to be showing rejection. If you spend the most time with your worst performers, then the message you are sending to those employees is that "the better your performance becomes, the less time and attention you will receive from me, your manager."[9]

Buckingham and Coffman make the important point that spending time with team members before and after investing in their development and growth, whether a training class or training program or one on one coaching program, will increase your chances of knowing whom to spend more time with and who may have a performance issue. Where these authors missed the mark in my humble opinion, is in setting team members up to inventory their strengths and thus, so called weaknesses. The moment we as leaders begin to identify where someone is weak, we ping an additionally basic human need and if negative, impediment: self-worth and self-image.

The attention paid to an employee by a manager or soon to be leader, develops behaviors in ways that you may not realize, as does your focus on the growth of those team members. Should your company not offer internal training or fund vendor-led training programs offered internally or externally, there are a number of educational institutions that provide corporate universities, learning bursts, webinars, and training. Many of them will come to your site, customize a program, and reduce the cost of training for your company by instituting a college credit program. There are also several training firms and companies that provide valuable training and development, such as Contagious Companies, Inc., Ken Blanchard companies, or the Center for Creative Leadership. Each have their own feel and flavor and focus. Contagious Companies, for example, focuses specifically on those managers who've been promoted, but not prepared, and develops their leadership through live classroom and webinar training, coaching, and consulting with the senior executives on job fit analysis and role clarity.

A Word on Contagious Companies, Inc.

Contagious Companies, Inc was founded in 2003 by the author of the very book you're reading. It is a five-division training and consulting firm focused on helping managers who've been promoted, but not prepared. The way in which we help those managers includes live training, online training, webinars, coaching, consulting and assessments. Each program is tailored to meet the needs of those leaders in attendance and often it is a combination of services that successfully prepares managers for effective leadership. more information may be found at www.ContagiousCompanies.com or by calling 1-866-382-0121.

Three Little Expectations

It has been said that the greatest managers believe that if you expect the best from people, then more often than not, the best is what you get.[10] What do you expect from the employees paid to follow your directions? Have you shared your expectations with them? Do you expect them to grow? You may be interested in their growth, but have you told them so? Do they know in what way you expect them to grow? When once I served as a regional manager of training for a sizeable telecommunications company, I chose to clarify my own answers to those questions and share with the team I had the privilege of leading, my own expectations. Perhaps I preferred short and sweet even back then because even with significant thought, there were only three. I didn't have many, and actually the need to make such a list grew out of question asked of me by a close friend and colleague. "What is your passion?" he said. "What is your personal signature?" Both seemed appropriate questions for both the PERSONAL ME and the MANAGER ME that I was trying to be in the beginning. But, as a result of these questions, I decided one signature characteristic of mine would be to have clear and consistent expectations for each person who reported to me, as this area is often neglected. Many employees report spending great amounts of time wondering what is expected of them. The fact that I did it, isn't reason enough for you to do the same. Keeping my own list shortened to three doesn't mean your own list needs to be less than thirty. This is simply a guide or one example to help you create your own, in an area where a blank slate can, at times, be a detriment.

Three Little Expectations

- Engage in Active Learning

  - Feedback and Follow Through

  - Have a Life

Engage in Active Learning Means...

When a new member joins a team I have the privilege of leading, he or she learns of these expectations within the first two conversations. The intent is to show these expectations are as important to the employee, and to me, as the basic job responsibilities. First, I ask employees to engage in active learning; to look always for ways to learn new information about the industry they are in and the job they're doing, or the customers they will serve or are serving. This expectation can also prompt a number of new questions. Are there others who do it better, or differently? Are there others within our own company from whom they can learn? What do our customers have to teach us? What do our competitors have to teach us? Learning the answers to these and more questions, is fundamental to growth. Knowing that my expectation is for each person to learn regularly, particularly when our focus is on the adult learning and training industry, sends a clear message. Perhaps you also align your expectation with your industry, either in words only or in what you are asking of each team member. The additional, initially unintended, message is that mistakes are permitted here and learning from them is encouraged.

Those in a constant state of learning, who make mistakes and try new things and are usually better for it, if they are allowed to make those mistakes, and experience the following growth period. Making a mistake is, in fact, one of the best ways to learn. It may be painful and even seen as a failure by some. But, those who stay mired in the failure stage will not readily learn from their mistakes, often destined to repeat them. The first step after the failure is where the learning comes in and that is what I encourage: that first step after and the growth that occurs during that step, as opposed to repeated mistakes of the same event. Just as, when a new horse-back rider takes a bad fall, he is told to get back on the horse and try again, I ask employees to dust themselves off, learn from the experience, and carry on. Thankfully at work, broken bones are rarely the consequence of a "fall" in the workplace.

Ever learn something and do it perfectly every time there after? Only a small percentage would answer yes to that question. For most the answer is nope. But there are those managers who have forgotten the first time they learned a new skill or practiced a new technique or behavior. They continue to act as if they have always known how to ride a bicycle but have long since forgotten the period of time when it involved training wheels. They often seem to believe they've always acted from the benefit of years of prior experience. This misperception, or belief, comes from the fact that it is darn hard to unlearn something. Once you learn a new skill or new technique, based on neuroscience, it sticks with you. The habit may become dusty or less fluid from lack of practice but pick it back up and it will take mere moments to regain the hang of it.

Allow the folks who report to you to make a few blunders, for these and other reasons. Let them make minor mistakes and learn from them. Pick them up, dust them off, show or tell them a better way and let them go forward. The chapter on forgiving mistakes goes into much greater detail and talks through just how many times you share such forgiveness. Just remember that the amount of forgiveness you provide to employees directly correlates to the amount of leeway and forgiveness they will share with you on your next great oversight. Not that leaders ever make those, much less the same mistake over and over, right? .

Give Feedback and Follow Through Means...

Feedback and follow-through, my second expectation, is requested from each team member, to each team member, to each customer, for each customer, on each commitment, and then back to me as necessary. I have gone so far as to alert employees to the fact that I expect them to share respectful feedback with me if they have a more efficient process for doing something that I spend a lot of time with, or if I say something and it comes out much differently than they think I meant it. (Even the best managers occasionally use the tone of Godzilla when operating under stress and fatigue.)

There have actually been two people who courageously shared with me that they thought I just "bit their head off" and asked if that was my intention. They were very respectful and tried to be humorous and tactful with their question. Because of my expectation, their question was welcome and caused me to stop and laugh for a moment and realize that I needed to lighten up a bit. I promptly apologized, redirected my frustration at the situation we were in, instead of the people in it with me, and rephrased my comments and expressions in a way that was less caustic. I have great respect for each of these employees who followed through on their commitment to give feedback. I believe, and have heard, that their respect for me increased upon my allowing their feed- back on my delivery. Had I chastised the employee for sharing this feedback with me, this would have sent a mixed message and given the wrong attention to the right behavior. Reinforce whatever expectations you are looking for. Set the example by following through.

In many cultures a man's (or woman's) word is a bond. So, no matter where you live, chances are that doing what you say you will do still has great value. Follow-through—doing what they said they would do—is requested of all team members for the purpose of increasing credibility, displaying of integrity, and creating more exposure. If I am interested in the growth of these employees, I want them to look good, both for themselves and for the team that I am supervising, and for others to have a high opinion of their actions and behaviors. I also want them to learn the value of doing what one says. It is a small habit that can produce big results. That is why I expect it from each team member.

Life Balancing Act

One more deceptively small concept that can produce big results is balance, or what I refer to in my expectations as *having a life*. Simple words and a fairly simple concept when dealing with weights and a scale, yet much more difficult when the weights are seen as people and the scale is life. Balance can be described in one sentence, as those who have worked with me can attest. "If you don't have a life, go get you one before you start this position." An employee with a balanced life will be much more interested in enriching the many different sides of work and life. Those without balance will burn out one side, work life or personal life, and be of little use to you, your company and possibly themselves, until they become balanced again. The idea is to maintain a consistent balance, which will be covered in more detail in Chapter 4. However, remember, that reference to balance really being better designed for a scale. Shortly we'll reveal what is far more effective to be seeking.

Each of these three expectations remains in the background. They serve as the backdrop for all meetings, activities, and new initiatives on the team. They are not used as a quiz topic, except when a new person joins the team, and they are not a mantra that we all chant when we are together. They provide clarity in areas where the employees are asked to use their best judgment. They provide a foundation for how we conduct business. Whatever your expectations are, even if they differ from the ones that I have provided, they will serve a similar purpose if you make them clear to yourself and then clearly share them with those who report to you and with those you have the privilege of leading. The guidelines that you provide to "empower" employees are of paramount importance and will allow them to grow into better decision-makers for similar situations. Information, communication, and direction are critical factors for growth. Clearly sharing your expectations includes all three factors.

> **Share your expectations or you will be sharing your feedback on failure and how to fix it.**

Mix, Pour and Create a Foundation

Once you have sought out the development opportunities available in your organization, availed the employees on the team you manage of these opportunities, and shared with the team your expectations for their behavior, you just sit back and wait. Think so? The last house I watched being built did not magically build itself once the foundation had been poured. Growth is a continuous building process and one that benefits from regular pruning, trimming, and directing.

Asking employees to set and monitor progress, by setting goals and measuring achievement, is another way to nurture this process and give some direction. Lest you believe that I am saying you can "grow" people, much as you grow trees and plants, allow me to clarify. Ask each employee to set goals. Show them a set of guidelines they can use, such as the acronym often used in goal-setting: SMART. Each goal works best if it is Specific, Measurable, Attainable, Recorded, and Timed, the words used to represent each letter in the SMART acronym. Teach employees a goal method and then how to monitor their own progress. Your encouragement will help them grow, along with the clarity of the goal that has their focus.

One method found very successful is to request a combination of goals. Ask each employee to share with you in writing (Recorded) one professional and one personal goal that outlines exactly (Specific) what they want to achieve, have, reach, be, or attain over the next quarter, half year or year. (I have often asked for a personal goal to help me gain additional insight into the person and his unique quality or desires as an individual.) Each goal is then written with a timeline (Timed) and is stored in the employees' file. As a leader, your role entails helping that team member to be reassured where they struggle with the measure of whether or not a goal feels attainable. Be very aware that what may be unattainable for you is within reach for someone who truly believes it can be done. Exercise caution on deeming a goal valid for someone else and when in question, focus on measurability. Also share with each person that none of her goals, professional or personal, will be shared with other members of the team, unless team members can assist in the accomplishment of them, and then only with her explicit permission.

The measurement piece determines how will the team and the goal setter know when to celebrate? (Measurable) How will you both celebrate when the milestone reaches achievement? Is it a goal that is probable, or even possible? (Attainable) I mention this again, because a leader's judgment of a person's goals, who is bearing their soul or vulnerable desire, is tricky and happens inadvertently with long term negative impacts. For example, if the goal-setter has declared a desire to become the CEO, reinforce the ambition, as this is certainly possible in most cases and at some point, and in some company. Focus more on a plausible timeframe for that person. However, if the goal-setter declares that he would like to remodel the office and begin knocking down walls during budget cutbacks—well, you get the idea. The important thing is to set them up for success in reaching their goal and to also be mindful or how susceptible and sensitive most adults are to criticism and judgment.

When it comes to goal establishment, I am less concerned about the personal goal, qualitatively. Over the years, I have seen personal goals range from owning a Harley, to losing ten pounds, to becoming a parent, and many others. And while this information helps me better understand the wants, desires, and potential points of balance for each employee, it does not warrant my judgment or comment, in any other way than to ask if it is specific, measurable, attainable, recorded and timed. Personal goals are just that, personal, and they provide me with a glimpse into who the employees are and wish to become. If they wish not to share personal information, the process of my leading that individual's progress may impeded, but not derailed and this is an area I will often refer to their coach, if we've engaged one.

Business coaching does and should, focus on both the personal and the professional goals as coaching really addresses the behavior of the entire person. Coaching as a leader will nearly always lean toward work as leaders rarely have the time to devote to delving into the personal life of an employee. However, business coaches are specifically for the one on one development of an important part of your business and are extremely helpful when you find a team member either with tremendous potential, or barriers in their own way, or in need of rapid development that will take more time than the leader has available.

Professionally Speaking

Going back to the professional goal, however, this one warrants the leader's immediate attention, as it is the responsibility as a manager and leader to assist in achieving this professional goal in any way possible. If I am interested in the employee's growth, and achieving goals is a form of growth, then I need to be all over how to help make this happen. If you use the SMART method and the collection of goal information, a review of the professional goals, coupled with guidance, will show your interest in the employee's growth. One model to follow is twice a year, have the employee meets with you and review his goals and his progress toward them thus far. There is, of course, always the option for revision. This exercise is much more about learning how to write goals, follow their progress, and feel a sense of achievement, than about setting a statement in stone and holding the author accountable despite change of heart or insurmountable obstacles. Growth includes changes of heart when a shift feels needed and the inclusion of new skills or interests. Professional goals are subject to change at the request of the employee and the leader.

During the review of professional goals, you may find a statement of desire for promotion or career development or change. Listen to those. Pay close attention to what is not explicitly written. A goal from your top performer that indicates he has a dream of becoming a writer may let you know that he is not in this position for a long-term career. On the other hand, it may indicate that he would be the best person to edit the company newsletter. The professional goals of any one of the employees on the team you manage may align with a career path that extends from her current position. In fact, at one time I led a team of trainers who were in their dream job. All of them were passionate about training and maintained career goals that would make them better trainers over a long and hopefully prosperous career. Not all employees, or leaders, share this enthusiasm.

When an employee's goals reflect a desire to grow out and away from the current position, pay attention and provide help. Be a resource. Brag about the skills of these employees to everyone you know. You are interested in their growth, almost as much as they are, and that includes growth outside the department and even outside the company. Read that one again. Yes, growth can be outside the company, but why should you help with that? There are two reasons. Employees who leave the company, who may have learned from you, and who may respect your leadership, may recommend you for a new opportunity with their new employer. Secondly, the employees under your leadership are people, not headcounts. If another opportunity is more tempting than his current role, you will not get all of his productivity in his current role at any point, so find a new place for him to focus so you can find the ideal candidate who will be passionate about that position. Support what works best for the people you are trying to lead when it comes to goals. It will pay off exponentially, for you and for them.

Get More Than You Pay for and Then Some

There are a dozen resources on goal setting, goal writing and even goal achievement. Many have set forth the steps clearly and given insight into the ability to achieve the most unimaginable goals using the SMART steps, though there are dozens of names for goal models. One author who walked me through this process when I was very young is Joe Karbo. His book, *The Lazy Man's Way to Riches*, is a quick read and may give you more value than you paid for it. In fact, make that ten times more value. The clarity alone of what you're really after will propel you in a new or renewed direction. I encourage you to seek out more information on goal setting yourself, before you encourage others to do it. This is particularly true if you're not already familiar with the practice and process. The book *Goals!* by Brian Tracy is one of the best tools I have found in this area in recent years. If one of your expectations were to include learning new things, this could be an outstanding opportunity to lead by example. You will also, of course, run across the plethora of resources on the Law of Attraction and affirmations and vision boards. No matter how you think any of your life's accomplishments happen, whether you believe in energy or prayer or the power of green M&Ms, there is no resource who argues with one simple common fact about our own goals and achieving them. We humans can accomplish for more than we even believe, if we will get clear on what we truly want, and stay focused on achieving that item, action, or feeling.

Perhaps the feeling you are after is the one you'll have when called the best leader *ever*. Get clear and stay focused and remember the practice of management includes the process of reviewing written goals and articulating expectations. Leadership involves helping people find ways to meet their goals and serving as a resource for them and their efforts. Strong leaders even groom successors to fill their vacancy and succeed in other areas, but one has to know of a person's desire to fill your role in order to groom him or her for it. And, one has to not be threatened when someone says, "I want your position".

What Do You Care?

Do you? Care. Do you care about their growth and their goal achievement? Treat employees with as much interest as you would show a close friend, on a professional level, with sincerity and the answer to those questions will be a resounding, yes. Care about employees' growth, who they are, and where they want to go, and give them some guidelines, parameters, and tools for the journey. As a leader, you must really care, not simply make it look as if you do by going through the motions. Often attributed to Hallmark, the saying you've likely heard is that "People don't care how much you know until they know how much you care."[11] Think about that for a moment.

The original creator of the nation's largest fleet of GM cars had a goal to live her life in such a way that when she died, people would say she cared.[12] And look at the following that she had. There are over 8,000 pink Cadillac's on the road and over 500,000 cosmetic consultants for a business that was begun by a very skilled and determined leader, the late Mary Kay Ash, who cared about the growth of every one of the women who became involved in her business. Her motto was to imagine everyone out there with a sign around her neck that said: *"Make Me Feel Special"*. Who can argue with a motto that has the support of a whole fleet of pink people proving it to be effective?

Whether or not you truly harbor sincere concern for those you manage and their growth, is up to you. To be effective, you must be sincere. People will instantly see through insincerity if they are paying attention. I offer two notes of caution in this area. First, insincerity creates a very ugly reaction from some people. Secondly, if you try to fake really caring and are very good at, going through all the appropriate motions (which I recommend only if you have Oscar-award-winning acting skills), you may be surprised at the positive feedback you receive. I mention award-winning acting skills because those paying attention will not be fooled, but those not paying attention may be temporarily—until you make the transition from faking it to feeling it – lulled into believing the act. You may find that what you are doing becomes less and less insincere and more and more real with the help of positive reinforcement and knowing a few steps that increase your own confidence that when it comes to leading, you actually know what you're doing.

But, as a final caution, whether it is real and sincere or of the "fake it until you make it" variety, care about those that you manage and will lead, at your own risk. They may actually change from headcounts to people as if almost by magic. They may actually grow and change and learn, and then they might care back, which, in the event that you ever need help from them in your own growth toward leadership, may be highly advantageous. What's that? You would feel uncomfortable asking an employee you manage or lead for help with your own desired goals and objectives? Asking for help is human, but not all humans do it. Being human causes us to remove the

Super Manager (said in my best super hero voice with booming sound effects) cape and that is a problem unless of course, you want to be a super leader…

and if that's what you're really after,

then it might be time to master this next step...

3 LEADERS ASK FOR HELP

The concept of help gets a bad rap. In leadership, help can even be a sign of weakness or confused with a four-letter expletive. Successful leaders, however, know from whom and how quickly to seek out help from those with more expertise in an area than they possess themselves. The trick is being comfortable with not knowing everything. The next step is maintaining one's own confidence as a leader when the entire team appears to be smarter than the leader in one or more areas. With those two elements of not knowing and maintaining confidence well in hand asking for help from those you lead should be easy. For most, it is not.

In Corporate America, help is often misconstrued to mean delegation or giving out grunt work. Let me assure you this chapter is not about delegating to those you work with so that you gain help on a big project, can kick back, relax and still meet the project deadline. Well, at least not entirely. It is about asking those unique, talented, individuals who work with you for answers, solutions, ideas, comparisons, and contributions. If that happens to get you out of a jam on a deadline, great, but it's a bonus, not the main focus; even as being given a management title is a bonus and those who report to you are the main focus.

Help takes two. People, that is. Asking for help is simple, given the two earlier parameters. It requires a language common to both people and the ability to send a request and receive input. On a slightly grander scale, it requires the manager to have the confidence and humility to realize that a job takes more than one person, and that many problems are better solved when all or many members of the team are involved. Leaders are keenly aware that the sum of the opinions and inputs of many is much greater than the grandest efforts of one.

If the team you manage is not used to sharing their feedback or giving input, you will have to ask, maybe more than once. If the team you manage has been asked to help in the past only to find that it burdened them with more work, you may have to ask and then explain why you are asking. Then wait to see if they offer to assist. If not, try starting small and giving a good bit of benefit explanation.

Will Flattery Get You Anywhere?

Okay, if it were me right now, reading this book when I first became a manager, I would have to ask, "Why do I need help?" In fact, I asked this question several times from those who possessed much more experience than I and encouraged me to involve others in what I did. I discovered that asking for help has so many tremendous benefits that I now rarely hesitate to ask for help on a number of activities. When you ask someone for genuine assistance, they are usually flattered. This can also send a message that you are human and not "super-invincible-manager-man (or –woman)".

Revealing that you are human will not provide you coverage on the five o'clock news, but it will reinforce the fact that you make mistakes, are not perfect, must eat, sleep, and pull on your pants just like the rest of us. It will ultimately provide reassurance to those with whom you work, those with whom you set reasonable standards, expectations, and accountabilities. It will reassure them that you make mistakes, too, and that you do not know everything, which of course, everyone knows already, but which some seem to ignore and momentarily forget when they're given a title. As if those benefits were insufficient, one more reason to ask for help from someone is to make him or her feel special.

We mentioned flattery as a benefit; "special" goes one step further. Allow me to explain the difference between flattery and making someone feel special. Ask someone to choose the colors of the bathrooms at the newly constructed office and she may be flattered that you remembered her previous interior design training. Ask that same person to take on the responsibility of redecorating the entire office and help you by providing weekly updates, and you may have just made her feel very special, if she has an interest in that project and in taking the spotlight. If she does, then her positive feelings may improve her performance, increase morale in the office, and help you in your department in a variety of other ways. Remember all of those ifs and remember that if she feels overburdened instead of special, your efforts will have backfired. Different people feel special differently. Ask questions.

All for One and One for All

One manager I used to work with loved to ask me for help on projects because of my analytical, detailed, and perfectionist qualities. In a department store, these were wonderful traits for creating visually appealing merchandise displays. Of course, whenever she asked, I completely lost the ability to utter that cute little two- letter word we say so often to pets and children. It was as if the word NO had literally been sucked out of my vocabulary with that morning's floor vacuuming.

She would request my assistance on a floor move, (the rearrangement of an entire department), knowing that I worked on the sales floor and saw what appealed to the customers most. She would proceed to explain to me her ideas of where clothes and racks should go, and then she would—yep, you guessed it—disappear. Soon the department would be swamped with customers and I would be knee deep in a pile of blue jeans and bikinis, alone. This happened repeatedly in the junior's clothing department I managed. Repeatedly. And it taught me a lesson. Solicit help from those you manage, and then roll up your sleeves and act on their advice WITH THEM if it makes sense for your business. The disappearing act will quickly reduce any desire to help you employees may have. In fact, it may cause them to evaporate when you come walking down the hall.

> **When you really listen, you truly understand. Being one who truly understands allows you to become influenceable.**
> *Being influenceable is the key to influencing others.*

If you have a lack of knowledge about those who report to you and what they might be able to help with, introduce a topic and listen. Ask questions, involve them so that you can find out, and continue to listen. Previous positions, a knack for technology, caring for elderly parents, even coaching a Little League team, almost anything could have developed skills and knowledge that can be transferred to the current task or project. Better yet, begin by asking how you can help them. This may get the ball rolling and the request returned to you.

Once, when asked to help the training team rewrite four weeks of New-Hire curriculum, I felt completely unprepared. A four-week curriculum, consisting of a four-inch binder with seventeen sections of text and few pictures, was a mammoth undertaking even for one skilled in training design and development, not to mention typing. My manager at the time must have known that my ten years of hiring and coaching experience with new hires, my previous training classes, and my depth of knowledge about what a new employee needed to do the job successfully and effectively, gave me all the preparation I needed. Much to my surprise, members of the team told me that I proved to be a tremendous help with the project, even though my skills were not in the original job description. Furthermore, my skills when I finished the job were far greater than those I brought with me.

Many times, those you lead possess skills that are well- suited to a particular task, even though they're not clearly stated in a job description. You need to ask and observe and listen for responses. Have you ever assumed that someone would not do particularly well on a project because they did not have the stated qualifications? You may have been right, or you may have missed out treasures you could have found if you had only asked.

Through the Good Times...and Bad

The times when business is good seem to provide a plethora of volunteers willing to board the bandwagon of helpers. When business takes a downturn, the lines of volunteers dwindle. When the business environment evokes fear of layoffs, the volunteers downright vanish. Yet you still can, and should, solicit help. Why? Who better to ask than those who will be affected most? Adults like to feel some control of their own lives and destinies. (As if you were unaware of this little gem of wisdom.)

During a round of budget cuts and layoffs, I was told to reduce the number of employees by two. If I had not seen these employees as people, uniquely skilled and talented, who had been coached over the last year to grow into their positions and thrive, this would have been easier. (One hat and ten slips of paper, followed by a child's game of "eeny-meeny-miny-mo", would have resulted in the goal I had been asked to reach. Instead, I solicited this team's help. I feel I must preface this with the daredevil television show tagline "Don't try this at home," because this is not a strategy to adopt if you have not invested the time to develop rap- port with the team in this situation. You need to know that the team you are working with has the ability to handle the emotions of a layoff, while still being able to provide objective feedback.) This group structure was unusual. The team I managed was made up of three sub-teams, five in one location, five in another, and seven in other branch offices. One person from each of the sub-teams of five had to go. One of these teams of five that I had to downsize was extremely close, had shared social and professional outings frequently, and had all recently moved to a town in which we had just become the second largest employer by opening a significant call center. They had been through a life-changing transition together and had a common belief that everything happened for a reason. They worked as a team with no individual competitive spirit present that would sabotage the needs of a teammate. The competitive spirit, had it been present and aggressive in nature, would have completely altered how this was handled and the way in which I asked for help. Consider that your warning label before the instructions if you have a highly competitive team.

The morning after my news that a reduction of one per sub-team of five was necessary, I convened a conference call and asked the close-knit team I mentioned for help in deciding who would be the one to find another job. Their response was overwhelming. Team members said things that ranged from "You could not pay me enough to do your job" to "We will pray for you to make the right decision", but then reality set in. They knew this was an incredibly difficult decision for me and that it would affect the livelihood of one of their teammates. I really was asking for their help, and they rose to the occasion. I made it clear that the final decision was mine, but that any ideas or thoughts they had were welcome.

The next two days proved difficult, nerve-racking, and filled with comparisons of skills, tenure and performance scores. When it became clear that there was little substantive difference between the team members, we began to joke about hair color, lack of hair, height, and number of pets as possible decision-making factors. As the only blonde, I was able to eliminate that as a factor. Obviously, none of the latter was plausible, but the laughter helped to relieve the tension and allow us all to think more clearly. Members of the team began to visualize who would have the smoothest transition into a new position and who had the most to lose. Members of the team began to help each other determine the pros and cons of leaving their current role to join a new team and take on a different role with new responsibilities. The phone calls came in one by one, volunteering, or convincing me why one member of the team or another should not be chosen.

On the day of my decision, the team had helped me find a solution. They did not, and would not, in fact, make the decision for me, nor was that what I had asked them to do, but they each knew their input had been heard, valued and considered. The two phone calls I had to make to those that I had to let go, both on the sub-team that had provided help and on the sub-team that had not, were possibly two of the most difficult calls of my business life. This was my first experience with lay-offs. But at least on the team who had shared input, amidst tears and questions, all knew that the decision had been extremely difficult and that it had involved all of us. I had solicited their help because they were closer to the problem than I. Each member of that team also had an opportunity to experience a different side of layoffs: the human side.

What many don't realize exists, in those cold, mean managers who must deliver layoff news, is that very human side. I do not mean to sound sarcastic or as if I believe managers and employees are distinct species from each other. Quite the contrary. Yet so often managers are treated as if they alone made the decision to change the number of employees a company keeps or lays off, and as if the role of the messenger with the bad news is easy.

The employees who once reported to me and with whom I had the privilege of working now have an entirely different perspective, on that situation and on the leader, who worked with them through the experience.

The lesson is that people must deal with situations that are difficult. It is a function of being asked to supervise other people. Conflicts occur, lay-offs occur, budget cuts and take-aways occur, and leaders try to involve those who will be affected when difficult decisions must be made, whenever possible and reasonable. Making a decision in a vacuum can often be the provocation needed to create rumors or larger problems such as resentment or sabotage. Ignoring difficult situations might also get you labeled as a difficult person. There's a TEDx talk for that called "When Did We All Become Difficult People?". You might recognize the speaker.

Chief Mentor and Listener

A mentor early in my training career frequently offered to help me grow, by listening. While I asked questions, he listened. Read that again. When I asked for his help, he would make sure my facts were accurate, smile, and ask me what I would do if the roles were reversed. It used to frustrate me to pieces, but he helped me by developing my "gut", allowing me to practice decision-making and showing me how to get out of doing almost anything (though I am still not sure that is such a positive attribute).

He helped me much more by listening than he would have by answering my questions. Like many great leaders, he taught me how to fish instead of feeding me for a day. Leaders are often mentors and managers, and advisors, and great listeners, who did not become great leaders while remaining secluded in an office, while making decisions in a vacuum. They knew how to ask for help and probably still do.

Go Ahead, Ask

If done properly, asking for help can bring you one step closer to leadership. If done incorrectly, the effort you expend in asking will backfire with twice the force you put forth. Therefore, let me further clarify the concept. You should solicit help from those you manage and wish to lead, if the project or task you are working on will directly affect them, will still involve them upon completion, and will allow their feedback to serve as influence.

Have you ever been asked to research an issue or go to work on creating a process for improvement only to find that a decision had already been made and your work had been futile? Corporations, organizations, and managers sometimes ask for this type of help, hoping that you will arrive at the same decision that has already been made and that both you and the company will reap the benefits of something called "buy-in" (a popular term dis- cussed more colorfully later). Can we spell manipulation?

Reserve the manipulation for numbers, as long as it is legal and ethical, and use leadership and emotional intelligence (discussed more later also) with people. If they are not affected, involved, or able to influence, don't bother them with a request for help; instead communicate clearly what has already been decided. A leader solicits assistance from his or her followers on issues that will create direct consequences for them, for several reasons. The first is out of respect and courtesy. The second and third reasons are the desire to help them grow and the realization that they are in fact, closer to the issue than the leader is. An employee who eats, sleeps, and breathes something that will directly affect her is much more apt to have a viable solution to a problem, or valuable input on the better way to build the very mousetrap with which she spends her days working.

When one is intimately familiar with what works and what doesn't work on any given project, she is much more likely to be willing to assist and offer suggestions if asked. In the same scenario, if this employee eats, sleeps and breathes that same project and is not involved in changes made to improve or change it, feelings of unrest, of being undervalued, unappreciated, and possibly even disrespected may set in. These feelings may lead to lower productivity and sabotage, but certainly not to growth of the employee— or the project, for that matter.

Ask Only if You Can Use the Feedback

It is true that decisions are made every day, by bodies of management as high as Congress, that cause change for all of us and our lives. We become intimately acquainted with these decisions, but we have had no input on or in them, for reasons that escape my logic and that of many others at times.

The same is true in business. Management and senior leader- ship may make decisions, about lay-offs, budget reductions, reorganizations, job changes, promotions, project assignments, and even leadership changes that significantly impact the lives of employees, and never bother to pick up the phone or talk to each of those who are going to feel the change. Often, of course, such consultation is not feasible. So I am not advocating broad employee input on every detail of business. What I am advocating is the request from an employee for input, where possible and feasible, before making, in a vacuum, a decision that could have been open to additional input.

Leaders and managers must run a business and make a profit or reach the desired business goal. The need to run that business may require tough decisions that employees below this level are not involved in, but which affect them. It is those situations that the employees or followers of a leader are affected by AND involved in that are ripe environments for leadership to ask for help. A leader who solicits help from employees involved in a situation that requires improvement or modification, gains the benefit of a better mousetrap *and* the respect and continued loyalty of the followers involved.

And There are Those Who Don't Think They Need It

Many managers fail to ask for help and complain that they are overloaded, overworked and overwhelmed, thus not performing at their best. This is not necessary and can be avoided. It is as simple as asking for help, but great challenges arise when the motive behind this behavior is to unload every responsibility that is given to you, onto others. You are to ask for help to get help, not (1) to pawn off what you are responsible for so that you don't have to do it, especially if the task is unpleasant; not (2) so that you can work less and someone else can work more; and not so that you can look good and take credit for what someone else has done. When you are asking for help, be certain to take note of your motive for doing so. If you don't think you need help, take note of your motive for keeping the project all to yourself. There is a balance between dumping work and sharing work.

When you solicit help of those closest to the problem, consider setting aside the feeling that a manager must know all and be all, should be able to go it alone, and should have all of the answers. No one has all the knowledge and is all things to all people. Try as you might, you will continue to come up empty on the search for such a person or the gift of being such a person.

There are also those who relish control and like to believe that if they control it all, they will be able to do it all. There are those who can multi-task more than most believe possible (and has been proven!) and, in fact, are able to appear do it well. However, these types and many others often fail, by seeking to succeed at everything. What positive experience with teams can you draw on to help bolster the understanding that the sum of the parts is greater than any individual part? For years I tried to go it alone. I tried to handle all of the management tasks, be the favorite person on the playground in any group that welcomed me in, develop team members, run a business, cold call for sales, work with clients, and stay sane. Luckily, I got smart before I blew that last item in the list.

Control has a tendency to cancel out creativity.

I failed miserably in the total process and did a fair job of miserable performance in a few of the specific areas. All this while I had also seen the above-par, better-than-average performance a team can provide! I was simply unwilling to let go of the feeling of control one gets from doing it all oneself. Not long after flat losing my mind over all that I was trying to do, I attempted to delegate specific tasks to others. I asked someone to handle customer issues, someone else to handle the books and the accounting side of the business, someone else to cold call for sales, and I let go of the need to be the "favorite one on the play- ground". Or at least that need being met while I was in the role of leader. The need does still exist, as yours do, as well, but let's address that more thoroughly when we get to Emotional Intelligence and that silly statement that you're one person at home and one person at the office.

With the new mindset that I didn't have to do it all and that I didn't have to be perfect, amazing things began to happen; most importantly, I began to increase my own performance and the performance of the company. I found myself with time to ask for help and ask I did.

What if the Help Requires That You Ask Up?

There is a level and a point at which you can no longer look to those who report to you for help. They are able to work on the issues that they face and provide a new perspective on problems at the management level that you hold, but they are often unable to help you with problems that are higher up on the corporate or organizational ladder. This type of help can still come from those you lead. The difference is that in this case they do not usually report to you but may be colleagues or managers whom you may unknowingly lead by example. They may, of course, also be those who lead you. A webinar called Managing Up is also popular on this topic and may be found in the Contagious Companies webinar catalogue.

When asking up for help, the process and reasons are the same. Those you are asking may be closer to the problem than you or, better said, they may have experienced before the problem you are having now. Those above you, or simply those who are more proficient at what you want to do, also need to be approached with a sincere desire for knowledge, guidance, and assistance. Don't ask if you don't really want the help, as I recommend with those who report to you.

Two Rules When Asking Up for Help

1. If you want to be successful, ask someone successful

2. If given steps to follow, follow at minimum, the first three

There are two additional rules, however, when asking for help from those at or above you at a higher level, who do not report to you. Number one: If success is what you want ask some- one who is successful. Number two: If you ask for help from some- one and he gives you steps one through five of how to achieve your goal, follow at least steps one through three, then provide an update on your progress.

There are many who will give a first round of help and then wait to see if the person asking will follow their advice. If the asker does nothing in the way of the advice giver's direction, chances are good that it will be the first and last round of advice provided.

The "Go Get the Book Test"

I met a comedian through Toastmasters who was a leader in his field. He was a world champion speaker and winner of the Annual International Speech Contest some years back. By virtue of his win and his willingness to help others, he is still a leader in his field. He is often asked for help and guidance and input, and for these times, he uses the "go get the book test" before providing more help than the person is asking for. He tests each person to see if he or she truly wants the help, as the employees you ask will test you to see if you really want the help or are merely asking in order to be nice.

Following his success, he recorded an audio series in which he mentioned the "go get the book test." His instructions to anyone who called or contacted him for help were to go out and buy a specific handbook for comedians. Those, he said, who listened closely to his advice, also heard him say, "Once you have completed that book, then call me back for the next step." In his estimation when I asked him for the numbers, only three per cent of those who made the first call ever called again for his assistance or the next steps.

As an experiment, I learned his methodology and decided to take on the challenge and give him a call for advice. My request for knowledge was not about humor, but about book production and audio book production, as well as public speaking. As if I had written the script, when he and I spoke the first time as mentor and "men-tee", he gave me an assignment to get a book. It was *Money Talks* by Alan Weiss. The "go get the book test" had begun and I was determined to pass.

I trekked to the book store the next day, back when we had those, ordered the book, and within a week had it in hand. Step one accomplished. I began reading and making notes on the book and finally accomplished step two. Once I felt I could answer a sufficient number of quiz questions and had all of my knowledge ready for the proving if asked to display my knowledge gained from his instruction, I completed step three. I called him and boasted, "Okay, I have finished the book, now what?" He congratulated me, and as if we had never disconnected the line from our first conversation, he began to continue providing directions and next steps.

Each time he gave advice, I repeated the process of following at least three of the steps he provided. There were occasions on which some of his steps did not match my style, but most of the time, I completed the steps for the sake of the knowledge I gained, instead of the immediate result I thought I needed. To this day, he is still my mentor and to this day, I still follow at least the first three steps he tells me to take.

Fortunately, I was one of the three per cent who passed the "go get the book test," and the information has flowed freely and supportively since then. How many "go get the book tests" are you put to? How many times do you ask the experts for guidance only to pooh-pooh all over their information as if you have a better way or know a better method? If you really do, then follow your method and don't ask up for help. If you don't, then ask for help and follow the advice. And heck, now taking action takes a fraction of the time. Head to Amazon, download an e-book, download a podcast, hop on Google, or head over to YouTube. We have no shortage of resources and information in our current time-period for any and all leaders and I'm always impressed by those coaching clients who order a book or take an action I recommended before we even get off the phone from our session. What we lack it seems, is focus and persistence. Readily available intel at a moment's notice has lessened the strength of our skills in patience, risk taking, and sticking with something until it comes to fruition.

Neither mentors nor employees are likely to closely monitor your use of their feedback. What is likely to happen is that you will forget you have asked in the past, run into the same problem, and ask the same person for feedback on the same situation. That is an embarrassing situation for you and for them. They can feel completely unimportant and you may feel a little sheepish for being so forgetful, but what is worse is that you have not done enough work in managing your own affairs to have fixed a problem that you have now allowed to continue past your memory range.

The same can happen with requests of those you consider employees to do something, as opposed to helping you do some- thing. Have you ever asked someone to complete a project, and then forgotten to give them just one more piece of information and then just one more piece of information, and so on? Have you ever checked on the progress of an employee's assignment only to be reminded that you just checked with her two hours ago or late yesterday and that she has not made any additional progress since your last check in? Sometimes this is memory, and yes, it is the first thing to go (or the first thing to be overloaded in stressful times). But sometimes, constant checking and constant information- adding is not due to memory loss. Instead, it is from a lack of trust that the person you have asked to complete the assignment can actually finish the job.

Just as asking for help follows the guideline of "If you are not open or able to take it, don't ask for it," management also follows the guidelines that if you are not willing to trust, do not assign tasks to others. Lack of trust can lead you into the trap of micro- management and that is a big pit of quicksand that will bury you alive...

... if you let it.

4 LEADERS MICRO-MANAGE ONLY THOSE WHO NEED IT

Hopefully, the preceding chapters have offered more insight into the traits that make a leader and what one can do to make the leap from manager to leader. Though hope is not a good strategy, even in leadership. Hope is based on what you believe could happen or will happen with certain actions. One could hope to become a better leader and also know this is likely with key specific actions. Rather than learn those actions through trial and error, which is often what happens when managers are promoted, but not properly prepared, this chapter is a bit more prescriptive and direct. In fact, this chapter also comes perilously close to telling you what not to do, which is an author's "no-no". I use the phrase "perilously close" because the fact is, unless I talk a little about what you should *not* do, when it comes to leading others, the remaining information about what *TO* do would be unclear. So, let's get to it. Micro-managing is not for everyone, managers or employees, and certainly not leaders. Most advice for leaders will tell you *not* to micromanage others and most advice would be accurate, except in a few specific cases. A true, and contagious, leader must micro-manage only those who require it, and only until they prove they no longer need it. And, I promise you, not as many people need it as you might think.

Where Did it Come From?

Most undergraduate degree programs include some type of course in economics. Yet, nothing comes to mind from my own courses on economics that referred to the micro- and macro-management of people. It is true that many managers are college graduates and are now managing people (though I maintain one can manage only *things* and lead people) with the skills learned on the job or in school, but where did they learn those skills? In economics? Actually no, as undergrad and graduate programs now offer courses on leadership, but this wasn't always the case. Even so, leadership programs now are still less of a focus than the courses that teach the dynamics of a business and not the people who run and work in it. This is ideal if you plan only to interact with yourself. What if, heaven forbid, you must work with other people!? What if, heaven forbid, you chose not to go to college? What if you're an exceptional entrepreneur with incredible vision, but no patience for people? How would you know whom and how often and when and when not to micromanage others?

The terms micro- and macro-economics were used in my MBA and undergraduate classes to describe the perspective with which goods and services, and the supply and demand of them, are measured. Even at the graduate level, only further manipulations of these concepts were expressed. Leadership occurs within and around our economy, and management, whether of people or goods, is often enabled through employee supply and demand, as well as budgetary dollars. So, it seems fitting that a term used to describe the inner workings of our economy should also be applied to people. That is, if you are going to deny and avoid the entire conversation of how people are slightly more complex, don't fit neatly and cleanly on a budget line item and have needs that stocks, bonds, and bell curves seem to be missing.

Fortunately for all of us people, the correlation only truly works if that which applies to pork bellies and oil is also directly applicable to people. Let's face it, there's not much overlap in those categories and as such, there's little need to repeatedly treat people like goods and thus micro-manage their autonomous behavior. But, some executives, bless their hearts, still try to do it. Leadership is all about people, and management is best reserved for goods and services, or at least tangibles. Using this definition, a strong leader (which you will become as a result of diligent practice of all these lessons) will lead people and know when to manage the activities or assignments of those people. This is, of course, unless one manages inventory and supplies alone, in which case you have my permission to micro-manage the dickens out of all your paperclips and folders.

How About if You Start Monday?

Definitions aside, you and I both know the use of *micro* in the term micro-management refers to a smaller scale, a smaller view of actions and details, as opposed to a "bigger picture" of the entire process. What continues to boggle my mind is the fact that only a select few, and I mean a teeny few, individuals should receive such microscopic analysis, which I referred to earlier as the management of activities and assignments. The few that I would suggest to you are new hires, especially those hired from outside your current organization or company; those with serious performance issues that indicate impending release or disciplinary action; and those existing employees learning a new skill or technique with which you are very familiar.

To be sure we are clear on what that means you do with those small groups of individuals, micro-management by definition means to…oh, wait a minute, it's not IN the dictionary, or wasn't before 1985. The term was, as are many organizational terms (just wait until the chapter on communication), was simply made up and pulled from economics, as well as management, which is what was believed to be needed with people at that time. The word "micro-management" arose like a brand new and admired skyscraper in a sea of old buildings from the vast array of buzzwords created in the late 1980's. So, if you are part of the baby boomer generation, you may remember when the world was missing the words micro-management. If you are of a younger generation you may remember when the word was first used in place of something else that had only four letters. Regardless, try being micro-managed for an extended period of time and you might share these feelings. Despite that case against the concept and its origin, there still are three good reasons to employ what I consider to be stifling behavior and tedious observations with those who report to you. As if they were big, icky vita- mins, let's take our dose of these and then move on to what I consider more tasteful and productive behavior and employee development.

Remember, the two primary groups of employees for whom it is appropriate to micromanage, and only for limited times, is new people and performance problems. As with any other skill or behavior, there is a balance, usually somewhere between over-use and under-use, to effective micromanagement. There is a fine line between barking orders and giving guidelines or information. In significant ways, people express deep appreciation for not being micro-managed.[13] Yet the opposite has also been observed. People express sincere job dissatisfaction if they are not given enough information or guidelines with which to complete or even begin the job they have been hired to do. Micro-management of newly-hired employees falls some- where in between.

Hi, I'm New and My Name is...

Often an employee new to the job is comfortable about his name and very little else. Though the new employee brings a great deal of knowledge, she is often not sure what to do with it, what to work on first, where to begin, and who to go to for questions, much less where to put her purse, what bean bag to sit on, which snack in the break room is here for all the team, and where's the bathroom, creating a reasonable amount of discomfort is simply not knowing this information that others take for granted. This is normal; it exists in any new situation. Adequate training and orientation should bring a new employee up to speed on the "what" that is expected as a responsibility of the job. The manager must then share with this new employee the qualitative "how" these things need to be completed and conduct what is usually called onboarding. This will be new information and possibly a new culture or way of doing things for this newly-hired person, particularly one hired from outside the company's internal candidate pool and will require some modicum of hand-holding. The initial sharing of knowledge is then best followed with check-in sessions to ensure "on-track" behavior and compliance.

There is, of course, no handbook that says you must check in with a new employee to make sure that he is on-track half way through an assignment. There is, however, a method of transforming management skills into leadership skills that mentions being interested in employees' growth (remember Chapter two) and that would suggest checking in early on and often or giving the appearance of micromanagement. Early on could mean once or twice on the Monday that he or she came on board, once per day for the next two days and the Friday of that week. It could also mean every hour on the hour, but I think you will be hiring more talented staff members who may not need that close kind of monitoring.

The alternative scenario is one in which the new hire has turned in a project that you outlined; the directions being to bring a draft copy of your suggestions for next year's business goals. Your past experience tells you what this should look like. The person you have just hired also has past experience that tells him what this should look like. At the deadline, he shows you something that is on a blank word doc with no formatting and isn't saved or presentation ready and has no columns or headers, which represents his draft work as you instructed. You had pictured a beautifully formatted PowerPoint with all, but the final numbers plugged in and this wasn't it.

The word "draft" did not translate, and you did not check in early on. Thus, you have both lost valuable time and effort, but more importantly, the new hire who was enthusiastic and overjoyed at this new opportunity

Management is not about being a star, it is about facilitating the creation of stars. Leadership is giving the stars their own galaxy.

impression he's made. There's no one to blame, but the two of you for not clarifying expectations and visions. This damage to self-esteem can be long lasting, depending of course on the subsequent behavior from his leader, and it could so easily have been avoided. Help the new employee become a star, and then give her guidelines, coupled with sufficient room to grow.

Check in early or micro-manage new employees with the following:

Steps for Micromanaging New Employees:

- Clearly explain expectations
  (in as plain English as you can muster and preferably in writing).

- Ask for confirmation of clear understanding.
  (Ask them to express their own understanding of what you said.)

- Arrange for a third- or half-way-to-goal checkpoint on the first one or two projects.
  (Make time to meet with them on these first couple of checkpoints.)

- Provide constructive feedback that will help them perform better on the next project.

  - Recognize when to let go, not as in termination, but as in letting them fly on their own. (Trust your hiring decision.)

Even though they are new hires to you, employees who manage tight family budgets, buy and sell homes or real estate, pay college tuition, prepare complex tax returns, and juggle dentist appointments with soccer games and ballet lessons probably have, and can utilize, the wisdom and maturity to handle almost any work assignment, if they are given the appropriate tools and guidance. No one at home gives them appropriate supervision and empowerment. Often, they also get no feedback and if they're a single parent they're the CEO. Give them guidelines similar to what one finds available for tax forms, but easier to read, and then know when to let them work independently. After all, you hope you hired someone who was already performing fairly well as a parent, a citizen, spouse, or employee, elsewhere. All she needs is the new set of rules and guidelines to play by when working here.

Document, Document, Document

Even if someone you hired was performing well in other areas of life, including the one for which you are providing compensation, what happens when the performance slips to such an extent that it requires written documentation, one-on-one discussions, and potential talks of termination? The situation is very similar to when she was first hired onto your team. All of your documentation, a form of micro-managing someone's activities, must reflect proper training, attention, specific guidelines that were created, specific guidelines that were given, and tools that were provided to do the job that is now being poorly performed. In many cases, when the original documentation of what you have provided is not available, the process must begin again. The micro- management of a performance problem entails documentation, documentation, documentation and you must even micro-manage your documents, just as you would the activities of the poor performer. For your documents, employee files, and those people who are performance problems, it is important to know where they are at all times.

New instructions should be written and provided to the employee, followed by scheduling regular check-in dates and times to monitor understanding

Steps for Micromanaging Problem Employees:

- Clearly explain expectations
  (in as plain English as you can muster and preferably in writing).

- Ask for confirmation of clear understanding.
  (Ask them to express their understanding, in their own words, of what you said, and sign something if possible.)

- Arrange for a third- or half-way-to-goal achievement checkpoint on the first one or two projects
  (Make time to meet with them on these first couple of checkpoints.)

- Provide constructive feedback and clear notice about the consequence of the observed action or inaction, to help them perform better on the next project. Should performance not improve, make sure you have determined the appropriate reason. Either they cannot do the job, will not do the job, don't know how to do the job, or don't have the tools or access to do the job.

  - For each reason, the supervisor should make additional effort to ensure that obstacles are removed, systems are made accessible, or knowledge and skill is transferred.

and performance. The steps for micro-managing a poor performer, in fact, are almost identical to those for micro-managing a new employee, and for similar reasons.

A feedback session will be needed following each remedy intended to assist the employee in improving his or her performance. If performance still does not meet the guidelines or expectations, recognize when to let them go or find a new solution. (Recognizing a new solution may include finding someone else who communicates more effectively with this person, who can deliver the expectations in a different way, or coming to the conclusion that this person and his expected performance was not a good job fit, or anywhere on the spectrum in between)

You will need to follow your company guidelines and policies on your specific discipline process or termination process. And while the concept of micro-management does not detail specific policy guidelines, experience tells us the human resources and Legal departments do spell out these requirements. It is best that you learn first, then follow their guidelines or create some consistent ones of your own before you find yourself in a situation in which you will need to use your documentation in court with now mad legal representation.

The primary differences between micro-managing a new hire and an existing employee with performance issues appears after the first three steps in the form of feedback sessions and consequences. Part of the reason for the difference is the difference in the purpose for monitoring new hires and monitoring performance problems in the first place.

Often performance problems have existed for some time, and the manager is only now going through the motions to gain the formal evidence needed for termination, or the manager has noticed a decline in performance and is entertaining the idea that this may not be a good job fit. And we wonder why micro- management has a poor connotation? Let me be clear that, although the above two scenarios are common, they are by no means what I would call best practices, or the ideal way to handle performance issues.

The feedback given to a performance problem must include more precise information about consequences, especially if you are already in a disciplinary process and working with a human resources representative or other team member or colleague. (I highly recommend that you bring the members of your human resources group or legal group up to speed on your situation as soon as humanly possible.) Clear notification of processes and the consequences of violating those processes must be spelled out and checked for understanding (even though you might otherwise assume an employee remembers them from the Employee Handbook or early discussions). You must make sure that the employee understands and has rewritten them in his own words, and possibly even signed something that indicates he agrees and acknowledges.

When micro-managing a performance issue, be sure to closely monitor your own behavior and ensure the best leadership decision, as outlined in many places in these chapters. For example, it can be helpful to take things professionally, rather than personally. Shelve your own reactions, feelings and emotions and determine how to remain this person's manager, while not managing his every action, or solicit another manager or leaders' expertise in managing this person's behavior and actions.

The last step, or recognizing when to let go, is also a bit different. In the case of a performance problem, you may be letting an employee go from the company, instead of merely letting go of your need or desire to make sure she does it right without your close supervision and input. Side note. Did you notice the use of words "Let(ting) go" twice the above paragraph? Same words, with entirely different meanings—another shining example of the business vocabulary created and seen as clear communication in the last two decades.

The other alternative in this micro-managed situation is to realize that upon careful inspection and documentation of the process, the actions causing disciplinary issues are, in fact, a result of personality clash or inability to mesh. Have you ever met some- one that for whatever reason, you just couldn't work with, get along with, or seem to tolerate standing in the same room with? Hopefully it doesn't happen often, but a leader is willing to look within, in addition to looking without, before making final decisions with high impact.

Put very simply, one of the keys to avoiding unnecessary micro-managing is to realize that you cannot and do not need to do it all yourself and they do not all need to do it exactly as you might. Many managers and entrepreneurs tend to define themselves as Superman or Wonder Woman, thinking no one can do as good a job as they can when it comes to their own businesses or department or team. So many of them are blind to their own faults and thus expect others to accomplish what we merely THINK we can do. None of us is perfect. Do I need to repeat that? Understand what your weaknesses are, and make sure you are not gumming up the works by micro-managing or trying to do multiple tasks that you are just not well suited for doing. Also, confirm that your micromanagement is NOT a stress induced reaction to the way in which the new employee or problem employee is simply different. Only micro- manage those who need it and only until they prove they don't, not until you decide you can no longer tolerate their different approach.[14]

There Has to be a Positive Side to It

As you can see, only a handful of situations will benefit from micro-management. Were there more than a handful, there would be no time for other activities. It is a painfully tedious process to check on each and everything that someone does. If you have ever been around small children, consider micro-management much like the type of behavior you must exhibit with a young toddler in a non-childproof home. Eek! Where is he? What is he touching? What did he just put in his mouth? Did he just cough? Does he have a dirty diaper? I wonder if he can see that. What did he just say? What did that mean? Where is he NOW?

This same analogy is helpful in understanding how many employees feel when they are micro-managed. Will she ever stop asking me where I am? Does she really need to know what I am doing every second? Can I not go down the hall by myself? Are they really concerned that I get it exactly right or do they think of me as stupid? Why did she hire me if she thinks I really can't do it? And so on...

Most of the existing employees who report to you have already established a working relationship, even a reputation, in many cases, of the quality of work that they do, and give you no reason to closely monitor that behavior. You have already seen what they can do and produce, and you trust that their new work will be similar or even better. Adults thrive on this trust and thus it is important to develop it early on. But how do you know what that trust looks like? How will you know when to let go (the positive kind) and trust that what you need to happen will happen?

Letting go of Control

Calling all control freaks! Calling all control freaks! Are you reading this text thinking "Oh my, there's no way I could ever just tell them what to do and then let them do it on their own."? Is your only definition of "letting go" the kind which involves someone getting a pink slip? Does your mind swim with nightmares that "They would never get it right and then we would miss the dead- line and then we would have all kinds of problems!"? Then you, my friend, might be the problem standing in the way of trusting and being able to recognize when the employees entrusted to you no longer need to be micro-managed.

> If your only definition of "letting go" is the kind in which someone gets a pink slip, or if your mind swims with nightmares that they "would never get it right and then we would miss the deadline and then we would have all kinds of problems!", then you, my friend, might be the problem.

I will always remember the turning point in my life, when I decided that it was okay not to require that everyone use my path to get to the end result. I actually recognized that there were myriad paths, all shapes and sizes, that one can use to reach the desired result. It was then that I decided to let those who reported to me use their path of choice, and the results have not disappointed me since. I cannot take credit for the concept; I am a recovering control freak who had a great teacher

He had called me to discuss my new roles and responsibilities as a trainer in Florida with the largest wireless carrier in that area. We had developed a good rapport in the previous couple of years and I was grateful to him for this opportunity to relocate to another state with a promotion, new challenges, and lots of potential. When he got to the part where he described those who would be my colleagues in the curriculum design department, he mentioned a woman that I knew I struggled with terribly. She simply seemed to do things in her own way and in opposition to anyone else's way of thinking or doing. We had worked on a project together recently and the confrontation I had with her still stung like a fresh slap in the face.

I finally phoned Rob, my friend, mentor, and new boss, and asked, with as much of a sense of humor as I could muster, "How do you do it, Rob?" "Do what?" he replied. I went on to elaborate on my question by asking him how he put up with other people doing things their own way, when he had given valid and clear instructions that he had asked them to follow. He laughed, and of course I thought, "I am surely going to get fired for being so bold!" What he said seemed trivial at the time, but it has guided my behavior with every employee ever since. His words were "I really don't care how they do it, as long as they get to the desired end result," His explanation included descriptions of winding roads and highways that end up in the same place; direct communicators and analyzers who end up with the same conclusion different ways; and co-workers who don't see eye to eye on the same project, but who work together to make an end result better than the one they could have made individually. This is not to say that the means are not important, but to change focus from how someone accomplishes something to what he or she finally accomplishes. He gave several examples that changed the way I viewed forced direction from that point forward. In today's leadership environment that sounds like elementary rhetoric. In a world where multiple ways to accomplish the same outcome, from six different apps, exist in the palm of one's hand or on a watch that is smarter than all of us, multiple routes to get to the same destination should be met with "no kidding!" However, if you are a member of Gen X or younger, this may explain why your boss seems lesser enamored with your innovation and creativity than in you following his or her direction. There was a time when being creative was not rewarded, it was taught out of you.

I Let go, Now What?

With my new perspective from my mentor, it was what I did from that point on that made all the difference. I also ran across an impact-filled article from one of the foremost leading experts in the world on creativity, Harvard professor Teresa Amabile. In the *Harvard Business Review*, she wrote that if managers want to foster creativity in the workplace, they need to encourage self-motivation and recognize expertise. It is difficult to do this while hovering over someone's every move, and in today's average corporate culture is now standard practice.

She went on to say that the easiest way to match people with the right assignments, which stimulates intrinsic motivation due in part to the fact that the employee feels an inherent value and involvement in the project, is to watch how they behave while left to their own devices. Creative inspirations can come from managers, but more often from leaders, who offer challenges, freedom, resources, verbal encouragement, support, and time for new ideas to develop.[15] How creative are you when you are pressured with deadlines and a boss who arrives at your cube opening or sends you a text every five minutes to ask how you are coming along?

The benefits of leaving someone to his own devices, once you have delivered the guidelines, far outweigh the comfort level a control freak will temporarily feel while monitoring the same person's every move. I once worked with a salesperson whose favorite request of management was "Tell me where the ditches are, so that I am aware of the playing field and can walk right up to edge without falling into the ditches." He often got his question answered and was able to train his manager how to clearly define his ditches. It is at this point that he no longer needed to be closely watched, or micro-managed.

Part of my letting go was found in pointing out a lot of ditches, but no specific path to avoid them or make it around them. If you can clearly define the limits and let go of control of the project team members' actions at about the same time, creativity, initiative, and new ideas will flourish. In my search for examples, I have discovered little-known leaders, local leaders, and executive leaders who have mastered this skill. One story of a man who is a well-known leadership expert, who gave someone the freedom to be known, who was capable of being great, stands out.

Max DePree, former CEO of Herman Miller Furniture Company (a furniture design company), describes those who have the gift for defining parameters and giving space to designers, as *giants*. Giants, in his words, give others the gift of space, space in both the personal and the corporate sense, space to be what one can be.

One of his favorite giants was George Nelson. In the late 1940s the Herman Miller Company introduced George's marvelous and, to this day, popular line of residential furniture. During the preparation before the lines were introduced, another giant appeared unexpectedly in an exhibit at the Museum of Modern Art. His name was Charles Eames.

George worked very hard to convince both his manager and Max's father, DJ DePree, founder of the company, to write Mr. Eames and ask to add his designs to the Herman Miller program. Both DePrees tried to convince George that this was not a wise decision and that it would only diminish the opportunity George was being given. George remained persistent. It was as if George instinctively knew something that neither the founder of Herman Miller, nor perhaps George himself, was aware of. Charles Eames was finally invited to join the Herman Miller program. In the furniture design industry, Eames has since become recognized as the greatest furniture designer since Chippendale.

There are now more than twenty products designed by Charles and Ray Eames that appear on the Herman Miller website, *www.hermanmiller.com*. What would the revenue loss have been if the senior management at the time had not been willing to heed George's request? What ideas have you missed out on because you believed that only your ideas were worth pursuing, or perhaps only those ideas that resembled yours or were crafted as a result of your input? I know that I have missed dozens of ideas, opportunities, possible revenue streams, and possible fulfillment of someone else's dream or desire, as a result of this way of thinking. My way is NOT the highway, but one small red line on the map of any major city.

> **My way is NOT the highway, but only one small blue line option on the map app of any major city.**

Micro-manage only if you have to and only for as long as you have to and know that in the process of letting go you may find yourself humbled and asking for forgiveness of previous mistakes you've made by hovering over people. You have made mistakes, right? In this area or others? Think you will ever make another one? We all make mistakes. Being able to forgive is a great relief and a wonderful feeling. Keep this in mind when you have an opportunity to forgive others. Oh, and one more thing…The best part about making mistakes is getting forgiveness from those you affect.

Once you begin to learn to let go, however... my bet is that they will readily forgive you for any oversights that you may make as their leader.

LEADERS ALLOW AND FORGIVE MISTAKES

A World Champion of Public Speaking for Toastmasters International, Darren LaCroix, once told me his formula for success in leading an audience. He said simply, "Use the dramatic effect of a pause, improve your skills by watching yourself on tape, and be yourself." Then he told me the common denominator of champion speakers was not their high level of skills, but their lack of perfection.

I, of course, immediately removed myself from that category as the exception to that rule. I thought perfection was the way to be and was attainable. He then said, "You are not perfect." to me and the rest of the 200-person audience. I thought, *THE NERVE! He must not know me!* Then he said it again, "You are not perfect". Have you ever felt as if the speaker on stage, or behind the pulpit, was talking directly to you; as if the entire presentation had been crafted with only you in mind? Of course, and while sarcasm is hard to detect in text, references to my being anything near perfect are simply said in jest. But, wouldn't it be nice if we had some way to actually attain it instead of just constantly reaching for it? Perfection gives us something to strive for, but if it becomes the only marker for success and the only way in which we know if we're good enough, it becomes a bigger problem than most.

If you believe mistake-free perfection is the way to be, this chapter was written for you and may be what helps you to give yourself permission to be less worried about being perfect and more focused on being authentic. If you have already come to the awareness that perfect is not attainable, then chances are good you're a frequent innocent bystander to someone else making a mistake or rather, learning a life lesson.

Uh-Oh is Different Than So There!

The people you work with and lead (and love) will make mistakes, of all shapes and sizes and kinds. A mistake is an action or behavior done differently than the rules, laws, guidelines or instructions set forth for such a behavior or action. For example, adding salt instead of sugar to your apple pie recipe is a mistake and a fine waste of a good pie! Attempting to take your trusty Swiss Army knife that you got as a graduation gift through airport security in your carry-on is a mistake that may cause you to miss your flight. Running a red light in the company car while you are talking on the cell phone and looking for the French fry that escaped the box and landed in between the seats is a mistake that could cost you your life. There are mistakes of varying degrees and varying consequences. Yet for the most part they can and should be forgiven, particularly when it comes to the workplace environment and your efforts in leadership development. As no one is perfect, mistakes are a way of life and a way, if not one of the best ways, of learning.

We are given guidelines and instructions, rules and policies, recipes and manuals, and even documents to sign indicating we understand each regulation. If we commit an action or behavior that is clearly outlined as prohibited and we do this without knowledge of the outline, it is a mistake. If we know the rule and break it anyway, it is called a violation and that's a whole different level of intent, or in some cases better judgment. But, let's focus on those times when the people you lead make a mistake and it is fairly innocent. Some they make on their own and some you allow and in both cases your forgiveness is warranted so that they maintain initiative and a desire, versus fear, for learning. As an added side bonus, if you can allow them to make mistakes, as you know they will, chances are good they will forgive yours, as well. Unless, of course, you still believe you don't make any. Maybe it's just managers who make mistakes; Leaders must be different, right? Wrong.

> **Sometimes you're a perfect statue; sometimes you're a pigeon with perfect aim. Either way, you will have good days and bad, just the same.**

Pobody's Nerfect

Many people, me included, have suffered from the affliction known as perfectionism. Some personalities are more prone to it in times of stress. Some manage it better than others and some apply it in limited quantities instead of sprinkled on everything like a favorite seasoning. It took decades for me to embrace the phrase "good enough" with gusto and to truly believe there was merit in that concept. Yet, we have a generation of young people who were raised in a very different environment and are less prone to perfectionism and more likely to give up if the effort becomes too tough. Consider that generational difference in your workplace. Are the leaders of Generation X or even baby boomers, scratching their head in frustration at how a Millennial may see participation as enough effort, versus perfection as the desired outcome? Our culture shifted from a hard-work and sweat of your brow mentality to a belief that overnight success and front-line worker to Vice President actually happens quickly, without all of that silly effort in the interim. Our workforce now is largely populated by those who have had limited exposure to the development of skills such as patience, tenacity, and "stick-to-itiveness". These skill sets and beliefs are formed far faster when one has had to work for an outcome or advancement or an achievement. Without the work, that muscle has had no conditioning. The same is true of mistake making. Without the downside of messing up, being embarrassed or even a bit of re-work needed, the effort to learn and remember a new approach or new skill set and lesson is that much more difficult. That muscle, so to speak, has had no conditioning.

Yet, we know perfection is an unattainable goal for any human. What we at times forget, is the different perspective each generation has on that word and its usage. Boomers and optimists and those whose self-worth is tied up in creating only perfect outcomes, expect perfect, try to reach it, and often beat themselves up mentally for not achieving it. "Get over yourself," someone once told me as I embraced this perfect expectation, and though I did not heed those words at the time, they seem recently to ring true more and more. And then he went on to say "You are simply not perfect and very few people, including me, expect you to be." Let that sink in intellectually. Examine how much you're willing to admit the perfectionism you truly do expect of yourself. Then consider how what you expect of yourself must be coming out when you are working with and leading others.

Expecting perfection of those employees who report to you, does you and them a disservice. Expecting perfection limits your ability to truly lead an imperfect being you have the privilege and responsibility for developing. Expecting perfection, will also cause you to miss the opportunity to focus on their growth, show them respect, see their value, and leave the door open to ask them for help. Just a note on how one small behavior can limit your ability to employ leadership skills from the preceding four chapter. But, if you still really believe perfection exists, try expecting it from them for only a thirty-day trial. Once your trial is complete, email me with your secret and if you were able to achieve perfection. If you were unable to achieve such a lofty and unattainable goal, there is no need to tell me about it, just simply work toward "getting over yourself" and accepting that both you and the people you manage and lead will make mistakes and that is what can and should be expected. The real question then is what do you do with the information from those mistakes and how do you teach the employee and/or team to use their experience to do it differently, and hopefully better, next time?

People make a lot of mistakes: leaders, followers, managers, employees, and yes, even customers. We all do. Making mistakes, however, is not usually a pleasant experience, so we go to great lengths to avoid them. We'll fail to try, find an excuse to not participate, choose to disengage, blame or even sabotage, but just how do we think the most incredible inventions happen? Do we honestly believe Ben Franklin woke up one morning with the swim fin in his head fully thought out? (He invented the swim fin, by the way, in case you've missed that nugget of wisdom) Do we maintain the fantasy that Microsoft has fully vetted and tested every software release with no errors or do we know that buying the first version of the new Windows release or the first iPhone new edition is not the best practice? We know mistakes happen and we've learned to live with them and work around them, but we're also very quick to criticize the companies and people who make them. Mistakes provide such valuable feedback and are in fact a way of best practice in the area of software testing. Mistakes, no matter where they're made or the size of the error, are some of life's most powerful lessons. As the old story goes, Thomas Edison made over 14,000 mistakes in his quest to create the filament in the interior of what we know today as a light bulb. He managed to view his plight as 14,000 ways that the light bulb would not work, but many criticized and teased him about his consistent mistakes and assumed failures and lack of expertise. Think about this for a moment, these people would all be criticizing in the dark now if Mr. Edison had insisted his only option was perfection of his FIRST effort. We're quick to judge and jump all over those who fail, but what if as leader you looked upon those willing to fail as those willing to also excel?

Even more powerfully, mistakes usually occur at a far lesser expense than weeks of technical training. They are some of your lowest-cost learning experiences, at least usually and this is where being an aware leader makes an enormous difference. Spend time defining the guidelines that if broken by accident, constitute mistakes. Outline the number and size of such mistakes you or your company or department can tolerate. Once you have defined those elements, you can then marvel at all the benefits that come both from creating a comfortable work environment in which people can grow and learn, and try new things, (which is often done through a series of mistakes all in a row) and from extracting the lessons learned each time an action or behavior was done unsuccessfully. Organizations say they want innovation and creativity, but few are willing to take the risk of letting their leaders allow for, or even promote, failure as part of the process in discovering a new idea or method.

In and among the guidelines or parameters that you and the company you work with have, some hard and fast rules will be spelled out in systematic, clear language that has passed the test of time, the court system, and a dozen excuses. These guidelines are subject to little interpretation. Thus, there is little room for mistakes made against them. You don't say to a police officer that you did not understand what the black and white sign with the words SPEED LIMIT and the number 55 on it was trying to tell you. (You may want to clear your calendar for a court date if you use that one for a speeding violation.) Similarly, many would discredit your cry for help after a mistake if you broke a clearly stated and time-tested guideline or policy, unless of course you were new to the planet, or perhaps very, very new to the organization, depending on the error.

Suppose you hired an employee who was new to this culture or country. The guidelines that are in place or that you create, which you may view as crystal clear, are often are completely fuzzy to a newcomer to this culture, country, or sometimes even company.

Many of our unwritten guidelines regarding gender roles, responsibilities, as well as hand-shakes and eye contact, that we assume are clear to all in their interpretation, have different meanings in other countries, companies, and cultures. In some cultures, a female employee is not allowed to shake the hand of a male client or new co-worker, until he has shaken the hand of her manager. In some companies, the good ole boy system is hidden or rather disguised, barely acknowledged or discussed except among them; in many organizations who've recently made the news an unspoken culture of harassment has been in place and not being a part of it was considered an error. Whether the rules are seemingly advertised with poster-sized bulletins, or more unwritten, so that unless you are a part of the group, your opinion doesn't count, those rules, when left unclear create opportunity for inadvertent errors. And let's be clear, some of those errors are actually seen by many as the preferred method of behavior. The point is in either case, your company or culture may be very clear to you, but unclear to someone from "outside" or not in the know.

Bring on the Rules, All of Them

Different countries and cultures do have different rules. Different companies also have different rules. Heck, different departments of the same company have different rules. If we are to focus on the rules or guidelines that people break by accident, thus making mistakes, it is also important to differentiate between those rules and guidelines that are written and unwritten, known and unknown. Strong leaders have a clear vision and mission, which if well communicated and documented includes written and known guidelines. If the vision is to "satisfy every single customer, every single time" and an employee fails to go the extra-mile or even the extra inch to satisfy said customer, it may be due to unknown, unwritten steps or even limits to stay within when satisfying the customer. In this case, it would be important to make the vision more-clear.

What IS included in "satisfying the customer" exactly? What can one do to "satisfy him or her in each and every encounter or transaction"? What would be considered unacceptable as a way or means of satisfying the customer? Companies with weak managers and leaders, and even some with strong ones, often operate on a completely unspoken rule system, in addition to the ever-popular employee handbook or human resource policy manual. The unspoken rules, or unwritten rules, as they have also been called, can be more powerful and more fiercely enforced than those that have clearly stated consequences. Breaking unspoken rules often can have even more powerful and detrimental consequences over a longer period of time.

If the unwritten rule in the office is that the boss arrives at nine-ish and rest of the staff is to arrive promptly at eight A.M., and an employee decides to arrive at nine-ish because the boss does, that employee could land in big trouble, both from the boss and his co-workers. These consequences would be in spite of the fact that the rule is not written down anywhere, also assuming he was never told the "policy" upon hiring. Imagine how long those consequences will affect his credibility, promotability, and so on.

Or in another scenario, some incredibly brave employee, newly hired and possessing great promise, may appropriately, and with tact, challenge the decision (made by her new boss's boss) to take on a new client. Though the challenge may have been appropriate and based on well-founded evidence, no one told her that you simply "do not cross Mr. So and So". (the boss's boss) How much promise does she have now? But wasn't it merely a misinterpretation of the rules and guidelines? Was it not an innocent error with good intent?

And then there's common sense. The age-old saying has been "If common sense were common, everyone would have some". And yet, they don't. But leaders can even be guilty of failing to forget to add common sense to hiring criteria. Then they become frustrated when the person newly hired seems not to have any. The assumption of common knowledge and the ability to use it is dangerous, but when you find yourself frustrated at how someone could possibly not have known what you consider to be common knowledge, consider just how uncommon most knowledge has become. In a different generation, what you know may be unknown. In a different industry, what you know may be foreign and also true in the reverse. In a different position, what you now know may be news to those yet to be promoted. Assuming all knowledge is common, even up to an including the belief that everyone should wash their dishes in the breakroom, is a dangerous and potentially frustrating proposition and risky for your effectiveness as both manager and leader.

Sometimes we think people are failing on purpose or making foolish errors and mistakes because they can't read, or because they're stu...or rather, less than smart. Sometimes we assume they want to try to impress the boss with their clear understanding of what we have so "clearly" defined and written out, when they're version sounds quite muddy. What may be clear to one person may be absolute mud to another.

The simple, but widely ignored, truth when it comes to clear meanings is that though there is a dictionary, with thousands of annual new word entries, there are far more than just those definitions listed for each and every word we utter. There's urban slang, generational understanding, and even connotation. Then there's tone, body language, facial expression, context and punctuation, as well as what words are chosen at what time, with what pauses, and in what order. When you assume that everyone understands what you as the leader have clearly written down or clearly communicated, you make a...well, you know what you make...but often we still go ahead and assume. This is why it is an invaluable practice to ask questions before making assumptions. It is often with sheer and absolute amazement that I marvel at the fact that we are able to communicate anything to anyone at all. Different meanings, different interpretations, and different perceptions all lead to one confusing language of words, rules, guidelines and expectations.

People will make misinterpretations and errors and mistakes, and often it is not their fault. Forgive them of their trespasses and move on. Reason number one for allowing and forgiving mistakes: most people will not clearly understand the rules and the guidelines to follow, as they are currently stated or written, in the way that the author of such rules intended. You may wish to read that again. Allowing employees and people to make mistakes is merely another way of respecting their uniqueness and considering the possibility that your understanding of something may not be the only one.

Five Reasons to Allow and Forgive Mistakes:

1. Rules are often not clear understood or explained

2. Mistakes frequently lead to innovation and innovative solutions

3. Forgiveness shows respect for human, versus perfect, behavior

4. Forgiveness of others sets a good example for what is expected from others

5. You'll spend less unproductive negative time keep score and holding grudges

Remember, there is more than one way to do just about anything. A mistake-free environment maintains the status quo. It disallows any new ideas or new approaches that are born from accidents. As Charles Kettering, the American inventor once said, "If you have always done it that way, it is probably wrong". Mistakes by others create times for creativity, innovation, fast action, and change. Sometimes a mistake creates a ripple in the market or maybe even a ripple just in the office. In any case, many a mistake, initially seen as an incredible drag or complete bummer, has turned into a modern-day marvel and extremely profitable new product or process.

Steve Jobs and Steve Wozniak built their first Apple PC because they lacked the money, probably due to a mistake in savings calculations or just lack of judgment or effort. Either way, they didn't have the money to buy the computer-building kits that were seen as the "right way" to build a computer back then.[16] Several million people are awfully glad they chose to do it differently, even wrong, and make that "error". But note, that until the "wrong way" succeeds we call it an error in judgment instead of supporting the effort to create something better or different.

Reason number two for allowing and forgiving mistakes: They create an environment for creativity, innovation, change, sometimes long since needed, and the ever-faithful "out-of-the box" thinking. Without mistakes, trial and error, and perceived complete and total screw-ups, we would be without many of the luxuries and simple pleasures of life that came as pleasant surprises to the person who made the mistake initially. Be on the look-out for the pleasant surprises produced by those you have the privilege of leading.

Some People Would Rather be Right Than Successful

On the team of people or one person or office that you manage and aspire to lead, how often do you argue a point or stand your ground, more because you hate to lose than because you believe in your point? Do you even remember the last point you were fighting for or do you simply remember the fact that you won the battle and were proven right? Jack Canfield, co-author of the best-selling book, *Chicken Soup for the Soul,* has since created many a new product and book. His focus is on success and getting out of one's way to become one.

Jack describes in several of his works, a condition of many people who lack a high degree of self-esteem, who must be right at all costs when in conflict with others. These individuals must often be right at the expense of being successful. A manager who defends himself to the death with multiple reasons for why the mistake was made and had to happen and was out of his control, instead of admitting it, owning it and repairing it, is guilty of needing to be right instead of focused on being successful. Humans make mistakes, managers are humans. Employees make mistakes, too. Employees are humans, too.

> **Right out the time you celebrate the fact that you've won, you may figure out what all you lost, but you'll still be right in either case.**

Reason number three for allowing and forgiving mistakes (even if the person forgets to offer an apology) is to set an example for reasonable human behavior. In this case, likely setting an example for how you expect team members to also treat each other, without needing to form a line outside your office so you can sort out every disagreement.

Mistakes allow for humility and humanness. In team dynamics, humility allows for mutual support and admiration of teammates, risk-taking, a reduced fear of failure, and an increased willingness to try new ideas and concepts. You want humility for yourself as a leader and for others whom you wish to develop into future leaders. Humility in leadership allows the team to see that you are not perfect, which may also increase your level of respect, rightfully earned as a non-threatening, non-perfect leader.

Reason number four for allowing and forgiving mistakes, even from people who fail to offer an apology, is to provide what will naturally be needed when you make your first or fiftieth mistake or error that affects an employee who works with you, or a customer. Think back to the last time you forgot something from your office and needed an employee to fax, FedEx, or email it to you. Think of the last time you showed up to work without your phone or went on a business trip without the right documents or missed a plane or missed a meeting or any number of other human like behaviors.

Perfection is threatening and creates a great deal of pressure, not to mention an unrealistic expectation of you and yourself. Humanity and humility, I have found, are quite comforting and ironically liberating.

But, When is Enough, Enough?

How many times do you allow for mistakes? This depends on you and your company and your level of tolerance for individual learning curves. It may also depend on the cost of each individual mistake. Keeping in mind the fact that cost does not always equate to dollars, the best answer here is probably…it depends. (Don't you hate that?)

When you are working with a new employee, the best course of action is not to put him in charge of your largest account first, or maybe not at all, without some assurance that he will not commit an egregious error that causes you to lose this client. Okay, that seems rather simple. But then you ask "Okay, so how do you know when you have enough assurance?" This will depend on several things. Leaders from all walks of life have often cited their gut, or instinct, as a primary measuring tool. Some follow the guidance of Human Resources in their organization and others simply consider a three-strike metric.

Perhaps you have very mature long-time employees who know how to handle customers, show and sell product, and close the deal better than you yourself could do. What happens if they make a mistake? Do you think they're perfect or are they just very good at hiding it from you? One copier company sent a salesman out to sell a church a color copier, fax, and phone system. The salesman closed the deal and then left the customer's location without leaving him the receipt needed to accept delivery of the product. It was a small error that could have made the customer rather unhappy, but he fixed it the next day by faxing the customer his copy. Easily fixed. With long term high performing team members, you are best served by not making note of each tiny mistake they commit. Often, if given the tools, trust, and opportunity, they will repair it themselves and quickly. Long time employees are often in the job because it personally satisfies them, and they have an internal need to deliver certain quality or quantity standards, as part of their own internal belief systems. They will often want to fix the mistakes out of pride. Let them. Some leaders use gut instinct to tell them when enough is enough, some will use company pre-set policies or guidelines, and still more will succumb to pressure from higher levels of management to bring an employee "up to speed" or "back in line."

Personally, in my early days of management, I had a very low tolerance for mistakes and it only took one for me to say, "that's enough". As I became more experienced and more familiar with the art of leading people, versus managing them, I recognized that people are human and will make mistakes. I even realized that I had made a few and that these were my most valuable, most memorable lessons.

If you are looking for a benchmark, may I suggest three mistakes in the same area as an option. Before addressing it as a performance problem, allow for that employee to make three mistakes consecutively in the same or closely related area. Even then, the mistake type must be repetitive.

Another mistake that is similar but is a result of trying to do something new, better, or different is not considered to be repetitive, but rather a new beginning to a potential string of three. An example of this three-mistake method can be found in the call center environment where a written posted policy states "three instances of the same error within thirty days are subject to disciplinary action." This meant that if you were late three minutes one day, five one day, and seven the next, these were three instances of being late. But if you were absent, and tardy, and then forgot to clock out for lunch during the same thirty-day period, these were considered three different events, not three instances of the same event.

If you feel three is too many or are comfortable with not having a hard and fast guideline as to how many mistakes are tolerable, then create your own comfort zone in this area and work within the guidelines of…it depends. Either way, exercise consistent treatment of the same mistakes.

When Enough Becomes Way Too Much.

There is a tremendous difference between making a mistake and repeating it a couple of times and something most commonly called milking the system. Mistaking your directions for how to provide proper patient care because the charge nurse did not hear you or did not understand you or misread the chart is one thing. Using this as a repeated reason or excuse to avoid doing complicated or unpleasant tasks, such as emptying a bed pan, is quite another matter. (The next time an employee complains to you about how bad his or her job might be, you can assure them that it could always be worse!)

Managers track numbers, such as attendance and absentees, figures and vacation hours. Leaders get to the heart of the problem. If you find you are managing someone too closely because they are consistently making mistakes and your company guideline requires you to, then consider approaching it from a different angle. If you work with an employee who you fear may be milking the system and taking advantage of your need to let them mess up a time or two, lead her to the awareness that you understand her need to learn and appreciate her efforts. Then ask what she believes she may be lacking in the way of resources, means, appropriate time, or maybe even training. Continue by stating that her continued mistakes will continue to be corrected over the next two weeks, after which time her mistakes will result in disciplinary action.

In this case, her mistakes then become a documented performance issue. As a leader you have clearly communicated, asked for input, and encouraged development and growth. You are a leader, not a doormat. You manage the behavior and lead the person. If behavior is not corrected, you then also have a job to do with those who report to you and whose performance you are responsible for monitoring. Coach, counsel, or discipline and develop, as you see appropriate for your organization, company or workplace and then lead that person to either make better choices or work in a place that is more in alignment the choices they clearly prefer to make instead.

Forgive and Forget?

If the employee makes mistakes, three in a row, repeatedly, or one of every different kind, back to back, you will gain a lot of practice in forgiveness. Your level of dealing with or forgiving the problem must vary according to the number and size of the mistakes. Effective leaders will react in reasonable ways in most reasonable, as well as, a few unreasonable situations. Effective leaders who encounter an employee who parks in your reserved parking spot near the front of the building by mistake, who honestly didn't know there was a sign reserving it, much less see the sign, will respond in a way that is calm, perhaps humorous, and maybe even friendly. These leaders are dealing with the frustration of the mistake and responding in a reasonable manner. An effective leader with an employee who has missed an important deadline for a monthly report, for the second month in a row, with no unusual or extenuating circumstances, will still be calm, but will begin to talk about consequences that will occur if it happens a third time.

> **Effective leaders will react in reasonable ways in most reasonable, as well as a few unreasonable, situations.**

Even the star employee will occasionally let you down. Great, effective leaders are wired to view these times as the exception rather than the rule. They believe that if you expect the best from people, more often than not, that is what you will get.[17] And when you don't, it often helps to expect that things will improve or that you will be able to take appropriate steps to prevent continued errors.

Ineffective leaders criticize and chastise and provoke the employee who made the mistake to have what is seen as an unreasonable reaction. Dr. Tom Miller, author of *Self-Discipline and Emotional Control*, describes the behavior traits that each human possesses. He states that there are approximately 500,000 of them and yet, any time a person of importance to us hurts our feelings, rejects us, or gives us perceived negative feedback, we use the one behavior trait that this person has addressed to define our entire self-image. This causes an unreasonable reaction when we feel our entire self-image is under attack. Blowing up at the person who took the reserved parking space, perhaps out of feeling threatened or without power and the belief, if only temporary, that without power you are worthless, is an unreasonable reaction. Ineffective leaders are often those who possess less self-esteem and fewer highly-thought-of behavior traits than those who are more effective.

However, on the topic of forgiving, when in public, the best course of action over a mistake is to address it, and perhaps forgive it, later, in private. Mistakes addressed in a public arena, whether forgiven or not, are likely to elicit an entirely different response from the employee than those addressed in private. People fear public speaking almost more than death (well not really, but it often appears that way), and fear does things to the physiology that will inhibit rational, calm, and logical behavior, which when giving feedback or constructive criticism on how to perform better next time, is probably what you'd prefer.

The final reason, Reason number five, to allow and forgive mistakes, is for your own good. If you carry around with you the records of every mistake ever made by one of the people you manage and wish to lead, you are using up valuable brain space that could be used for other things. You are also spending tremendous emotional energy on things that will not increase your leadership, your standing in the company, your impression in your boss' eyes, or the image your loved ones have of you. Sometimes, if the mistake is not egregious enough, the very best course of action is, in fact, to let that puppy go.

One Last Thought on Mistakes

Even what you perceive to be a mistake, according to the standards that you or the company has set forth for the employees, may be an opportunity for improvement. If the employee makes a mistake and it can be rectified, it may warrant closer inspection to see if the mistake is actually a new, possibly better way of operating. Ask for input from the employee on what he thinks might be a better way, and most importantly, the reasoning behind this thought process. Be careful not to corner an employee on this issue, as that can create a nonsensical or improvisational answer said only for the sake of covering one's derrière.

Approach the request for input or feedback after the heat or tension of the initial mistake has died down to a dull whisper. You then have a golden opportunity to ask an employee any or all of the following questions:

- If given the same circumstance, how would you have handled it differently?

- How would you have done it better?

- Do you have any ideas on how improvements on this process might be made?

Providing input is a way of contributing, and people are compelled to contribute many times in order to feel valued and needed. Forgiving the mistakes that they are sure to make is another way to make them feel valuable and an asset to the organization. People need to feel valued and needed, as well as, special. All people.

Another way to share this with those you manage and wish to lead is to provide praise. It is easy to do and can be free, fast, non- fattening, legal, and effective—if, in fact, those you manage interpret praise as approval and a sign that they're seen as special. Ah, that is where it gets tricky. Are you sure that is what they need to feel needed? Have you ever asked them what they need? Not sure why you should?

Confused?

Keep turning…

6 LEADERS KNOW THAT PRAISE IS POWERFUL

Not long ago, a mortgage company manager talked with me about the recognition needs of the employees she was supposed to be leading. Her exact words were "Why in the world do I need to provide recognition to these people for doing their jobs without screwing it up?! Do I look like a babysitter?" And, in fact, she did not. She was a powerful manager of things, and a budding leader, with a few problem employees on her hands. Babysitting was not what I was asking her to do, nor what she needed to do as a manager, and certainly not as a leader. It just happened that the people who were giving her the greatest problems were the ones who were least motivated by money and needed a bit of a different boost. She didn't know what the different version looked like and certainly, had no idea how badly the people she managed needed it.

Praise, Recognition or Neither?

The words and sentiment of that manager mirrors the thoughts of many a manager on recognition. *Why bother? Why should I have to? It takes too much time, too much budget and too much effort!* But, employees are increasingly being asked to do more and to do it more autonomously without any more money. To support such looser controls and less structure, as well as larger teams and less manager interface daily, leaders must create environments that are both positive and reinforcing, thereby leading team members to greater levels of productivity and performance and far fewer instances of loafing and inefficiency.

In tight financial times, rewards, recognition, and praise provide an effective, low-cost way of encouraging these higher levels of performance from employees.[18] The use of neither praise nor recognition could produce the opposite results of slipping performance, drooping morale, and a wilting business. And though the words praise, and recognition are often used interchangeably, they are in fact, two different, though related, concepts, primarily in connotation, versus definition.

The Council of Communication Management produces an annual survey regularly confirming what many of us know to be true: recognition for a job well done is the top motivator of employee performance over both the short term AND the long term. You did know that, right? Or do you still think the big motivator is money? It can be for some, for the short term, but in the long term, it hardly ranks as one of the top five. What many of us do not know about the number one motivator is that praise and recognition can indeed be low cost, low-fat, low effort, AND not require a four-level chain-of- command approval process, which money, promotions and raises go nowhere without invoking.

> **...recognition for a job well done is the top motivator of employee performance over both the short term AND the long term.**

For our purpose here, praise will be referred to as a more verbal, intangible, and immediate approach. Recognition will be referred to as more tangible, physical and public. An effective leader delivers both and encourages other members of the team to do both, frequently. Effective leaders also look out for ways in which they are inadvertently rewarding or motivating employees for poor-performance or inappropriate behavior, such as spending all of their time with the one problem employee.

People do what they get paid attention for doing. Thus, even a star employee, seeking recognition or more attention, may begin to perform poorly in order to receive what is seen as special attention paid to those less than stellar employees. They'll do it even if the "special attention" consists entirely of developmental feedback or discipline. (One word of caution about this term feedback, another confusing term that will show up in Chapter 9. This term is often used to mean what should be called "constructive criticism;" this is not what we are talking about here.)

Recognition and praise are positive in nature, meant to reaffirm and reinforce, and should be delivered to all employees in the way in which they need it. That can be time consuming. However, all that's required to reap the grand benefits is a little investigation, a few questions, and perhaps a little good old-fashioned ingenuity.

Investigate, My Dear Watson, Investigate

How do you determine what someone needs? Why should you even try? The "why" we have only begun to cover, and will cover more in detail later, is in this chapter; the "how" is simply step by step. The first of which is to ask questions. Recognize that step? Your first task for which you'll be asking questions, is to determine an appropriate method and form of recognition. If you avoid the "cookie-cutter" approach to giving recognition, instead considering the individuals you are dealing with as unique, your recognition will be more effective. Observe the people you work with and think about what would motivate *them*.

Consider some of these questions. Will they respond favorably to recognition in front of others, or would a one-on-one conversation, voice-mail, e-mail, or memo make them more comfortable? If they are in an office removed from than yours, could you send an email that others would see, making the recognition more public? Would that be meaningful or embarrassing? Could your email be misinterpreted? Will praise alone be enough, or should you follow your praise up with some form of tangible recognition? What other forms of recognition would appeal to them? (Remember to also consider the life that the employee maintains outside the office, his interests and hobbies, what he does in his spare time, and what he aspires to in his career development.)[19]

Ask yourself these questions and then seek to find the answers. These questions can be asked during interviews or during semi-annual or quarterly "touch base" discussions. The purpose behind asking during the initial interview is two-fold: One, you will discover more about the person you are considering hiring, and two, you will be able to proactively determine your potential level of success in keeping this future employee satisfied. If the only thing that she sees as recognition and praise is more compensation and your company is experiencing repeated budget cuts, you may find it a challenge, or a near impossibility, to keep her feeling valued.

What also became glaringly obvious when I have asked such questions about praise and recognition, is that many people had no idea what motivated them. Part of your investigation will require a second step: Observe behavior and interaction. Observations of employees on the team you manage will help to tell you what they respond favorably to. If one team member provides high-fives instead of saying thank you, the level of recognition that she may need is probably low, but certainly public and intangible. An "Atta-boy" said in front of others would probably work for your recognition purposes. If another team member writes quick notes on a pad of Post-Its® and leaves them at a co-worker's desk saying, "Thanks for all of your efforts," this employee may prefer visible and tangible recognition. Notice what others do. That's probably what they would appreciate have done for them in return.

Three Steps to Determine Their Preferred Recognition:

1. Ask them, as early in their employment as possible, and then wait for the answer.

2. Observe what they give to others and how they reward others.

3. Test the results of Step 1 and Step 2

> (Another option: provide an assessment tool to determine introversion or extroversion. Introverts typically prefer private recognition. Extroverts typically prefer public recognition. Try using the CORE MAP® Assessment offered through Contagious Companies, Inc.)

All along we have crafted our lives by following the Golden Rule of "Do unto others as you would want them to do unto you." (Repeated just in case you have forgotten it) We do it in communication and have seen how it sometimes does not work effectively. What about recognition? Still think everyone wants the same things? The fact is that the person who likes physical notes and leaves them is showing what he or she likes best. As a leader, know that the more effective way of treatment of others is to "Do unto others as they would want to be done unto," Tony Alessandra's Platinum Rule. Observations will tell you what others feel is important and valuable because most of us do for others what we like, as many are not aware that there are other ways and preferences.

A third way to obtain the information you are looking for is to provide a profile or assessment that tells you the recognition and communication style and many other valuable gems of wisdom. This is especially effective if many of the employees you are talking with and asking questions of do not know what motivates them or what they find valuable in the way of praise or recognition.

Profiles and assessments come in many colors and can be short or lengthy, administered by you or by an outside company, virtually cost-free or rather costly. Check into each tool and know that the most popular such a Disc, or Myers Briggs® often provide just enough to be dangerous. Much as when you simply ask what someone prefers in the way of recognition, when you ask them who they are in an assessment, 54% of the population doesn't know themselves well enough to self-report. Dig deeper and reach for more comprehensive tools such as the CORE Multi-Dimensional Awareness Profile offered through Contagious Companies, Inc.

The key element in determining what employees want in the way of recognition is to find out what they want BEFORE you make efforts to give them what you think is best and most effective or fits into your budget. Many very gifted leaders are very driven individuals who survive on internal self-talk and motivation. They require little praise or recognition. The same is true for those perfectionist leaders out there who discount most recognition because they see the flaws in their own work very clearly and assume others do the same to themselves.

Doing unto others as these individuals would want to be done unto would mean little praise or recognition and little motivation would be provided. In many cases this means that if the boss doesn't need praise for anything, the frontline doesn't get praised for anything. It simply is not about you, most of the time, it is about them. Ask them what they want.

Ask and They Shall Receive, Right?

Okay, now what? You asked the questions, observed the behavior and even doled out dozens of feedback forms at their request. The overwhelming response is "We don't get enough praise and we need X." Remember that old saying "Ignorance is bliss?" Do not ask if you do not want to know. Once you have asked the questions and showed interest, you must follow up and at least provide some semblance of what they are telling you they need, or they may not tell you anything else ever again, at least not truthfully. This is not the campaign of the week. If you are sincere, you may have to prove it, especially if you or your company has initiated a few campaigns in the past that never went anywhere or amounted to any motivation.

If they have identified praise as the number one need, then you begin to verbally thank and point out those that have done an excellent job. Many times, the effort alone of simply asking this type of person how they wish to be recognized, will gain you serious ground. Other forms of praise that are intangible, inexpensive, and can be done by you or the team are plentiful. Here are a few ideas:

- Call an employee into your office just to thank him or her; don't discuss any other issue.

- Volunteer to do another person's least desirable work task for the day.

- Answer the person's telephone for a day.

- Have the senior manager or company president call the employee and say thank you for a job well done.

- Tell the employee how good you feel about what they did right and how it helps the organization.

- Give the employee credit in front of others when discussing the work he did.

- Ask five people in your department to go up to the person sometime during the day and say [Your name] asked me to thank you for [the task or achievement].[20]

- Allow one person who has done exceptionally well to be the leader [if he or she enjoys this role] on the next project.

If, instead, you discover that the employees are seeking tangible recognition for their good work, you can be creative and still come in under budget. Here are a few tangible, visible signs of recognition and appreciation:

- Provide a 10,000 Dollar Bar, or Pay Day Bar, or a Millionaire Bar as a trophy.

- Institute a pass-around plastic trophy that the person who does well keeps in her work area until it is reassigned to the next honoree.

- Award dinners for two for doing something special.

- Name a parking or other space after an employee and put up a sign. (The Jenny Smith hallway, for example.)

- Provide Bravo post-cards or small notes that can be posted saying "good job."

- Get a *Lead Outside the Box* with note pads, certificates, and tip sheets on how to use the recognition tools contained inside it. (www.leadoutsidethebox.com)

- Cover the person's desk/cube with balloons.

- Buy the person something to use in his or her hobby.

- Buy the person something for his or her child.

- Arrange for the employee to have lunch with the company president.

- Bring the person bagged special lunches for a week.

- Authorize managers or other employees to walk around with lunch coupons that they can award on the spot.

- Make a thank-you note by hand.

- Inscribe a favorite book as a gift.

- Tape a candy bar in the middle of a long report and attach a note that says "Half-way there!"[21]

Many of these ideas and at least 900 or so more can be found in *1001 Ways to Reward Employees*, by Bob Nelson. If you are not a creative soul, but still have the heart of a leader who means well and wants to provide appropriate recognition and praise, find this book. I have referred to it successfully for new ideas on many occasions.

Tried and True, or False and Tired?

There are still the ever popular and often over-used ideas of bonuses, management by objectives, additional vacation time, paid days off, additional benefits, flextime, and others. However, with over a million lay-offs having occurred in the last nearly two decades, it is unlikely that your company is swimming in disposable profit that can be applied to hefty expenditures that most managers view as a nice-to-have, instead of a necessity. Let's face it, rent on the building is a necessity; paid days off because we can think of no other way to recognize an employee is not.

And some employees come to work to escape the life they have at home. Ever think about that?

The other amazing fact about financial incentive is that it is not the most important incentive. In the grand scheme of performance motivators, compensation is last, while goals, standards, feedback, praise, and means to do the job all rate higher. Please know that money CAN be a motivator, for the very short term, but it does not work over the long term. If you think money is a motivator for everyone over lengthy periods of time, the simple answer is "That is false", completely.

When employees receive quarterly bonuses among managers and employees, based on company performance and department goal attainment, the expectation becomes that this bonus arrives on schedule at a certain amount, every quarter or bonus period. Sadly, this expectation leads to employees writing checks on what they have calculated the bonus to be and four or five days before they know it will hit the bank with direct deposit. Often the company's direction on budget has changed at the last minute and the bonuses are not what is expected. Neither is the employee resentment.

The motivating bonuses have become a demoralizer in most cases, and over the long term, employees and managers see little to no added value in these. They are a part of the expected pay and not excessively motivating. But it remains a tried and true attempt at motivation that is instead, costly, false, and no longer working. Not the motivation you are looking for as managers or leaders.

The Choice is Yours and Theirs

Whatever you choose in the way of recognition and praise, in your quest to lead others, keep two things in the back of your mind. Number one: Most people are unaware, and simply are unable or unwilling to tell you, what that special treatment looks like because they assume you know. They assume you to be just like them in their thinking.

The second item to remember is a phrase we've already addressed: *People do not care how much you know, until they know how much you care.* And though this phrased has been used, over used, miscredited and used against some managers in an argument, give it some very serious thought. If that employee you had to fire knew how much you cared about him or her as a person, would the conversation be different. If that employee saw that you truly cared about her as a person, would she not try harder to do what you asked of her? You have no idea of the long-term positive effect of caring behavior at the office. Most people spend more time there than at home or with families. You will reduce turnover, increase productivity, improve morale, and potentially dramatically improve your bottom line if you actually give a hoot about those you work with and actually try to meet their needs, both in recognition and in all manner of leading people.

Just as employee apathy sends customers away, manager apathy sends employees away and does not a leader make. What makes a leader is the employees, or more specifically the followers. If you want people to follow you, find a way to show them that you care about them as people. One way to do that is to find out what they value and how they like to be valued.

But, I Still Don't Understand

One of my all-time favorite stories, that Jack Canfield tells beautifully, is about a mom waking her son up for school. He describes a bedroom scene in which the mom goes into the room and says, "Johnny, Johnny, wake up! It's time for you to get up and go to school". Johnny looks right at his mother, rolls his eyes and says, "Ugh, Mom, I don't want to go to school." And rolls over to go back to sleep. About ten minutes later the mother returns to the bedroom with a slightly greater sense of urgency and says,

"Johnny, Johnny! [Claps at him] It is time to get up and go to school. Hurry now, you don't want to be late." Johnny rolls over, rolls his eyes at his mother and says, "Moooaaaaaammm! Ugh, I don't want to go to school. There are at least a hundred teachers at that school, and not a one of them thinks I am cool, special, or values spending time with me. And there are at least a thousand students in that school, and not a one of THEM thinks I am cool, special, or values spending time with me. Give me one good reason why I should get up and go to school, Mom." Johnny's mother looks at him for a moment and then says to him, "Okay, Johnny. I will give you two good reasons why you should get and go to school. Number one, you are forty-three years old. Number two, you are the principal. Now, GET UP, and go to school!"[22]

If you feel you still don't understand the need for praise and outward signs of value shown to the employees you manage, reread the story. Schools can be tough, but your office is filled with those forty-three-year-olds who would just as soon stay in bed, then head into the office and meet you in the morning. Most people do not long for, jump out of bed for, or hold their breath for the opportunity to go to work or to see their boss's smiling face. It is drudgery for many, though not for all, and short lived for most younger team members. Though those statements are topic enough for an entirely different book, the point is that you, as a leader, can significantly affect that perception, if for no other reason than the benefit of your department of company. If you will find out what kind of praise or recognition employees need, and then deliver it in the way that works best for them, you will accomplish:

- Reductions in attrition

- Increased levels of employee satisfaction

- Higher scores on manager portions of

company-wide employee satisfaction
surveys

- Returns on your investment in them in
  the form of an investment in you and the
  company

- Additional interest in future growth with the company

- Significantly higher loyalty from valued
  employees than from those who are not
  shown they are valued

- Greater willingness from employees to take
  risks and try new things

- Increased willingness to take on more responsibility

- Improved teamwork and morale

- Less leader frustration and more employee bench strength

Should we keep going in order for it to become crystal clear that praise and recognition is an important issue? Or perhaps it would suffice to simply say it more clearly? I could tell you to build a straw man of how this would work in your office and to synergize with your team to produce results harmonized with the legacy and existing environment. Need translation?

Or, maybe we should examine the next chapter...

7 LEADERS SPEAK CLEARLY

Would you believe the sentence "It is not what you say, it's how you say it that matters," is true and can be backed up by statistics? Most would, however, in the face of email and text taking over communication, the truth is often clouded with the temptation of what seems to be a more convenient, more efficient method of sending a message. Leaders ensure they are both efficient, and effective, and understood with clarity.

In all of my years of training background, there is one statistic I've used in nearly every class that continually surprises people. Out of the entire meaning of the message that people, colleagues, employees, and your boss, too, get from you in a face-to- face interaction, there are three elements relied on heavily for interpretation and clear communication. These three elements are word choice, tone of voice, and body language. The importance or weight of each may not be what you think.

Word choice comes first in this list, as it is often considered to be the most important element, and yet it has long been said to convey only eight per cent (approximately) of the total meaning of the message. The second is tone of voice; it conveys approximately twenty-eight per cent of the entire meaning of the message. The third is body language, which conveys approximately sixty-four per cent of the meaning of the message. The numbers vary a bit depending on the source of your information, but never is word choice more telling than the others, backing up the old adage, "It's not what you say…".

If those numbers are true, and over the years they have been argued and debated, as well as deemed less solid than once believed, than what you're saying with your words is not nearly as important as what you do with your expressions and actions. This is true even of a text, which is all words, or so we once thought. Even in a text, it is response time elapsed, the number of times you can tell they are typing, emojis, and all caps that have tried to stand in for body language and tone of expression. Yet, with or without the numbers and in the face of an age where so much communication is conducted over a device or screen or without even interacting with a live person, the real questions for leaders are these:

- Are you being clear?

- Are you sending mixed messages?

- Are you setting a clear example of expected performance?

- Are you really listening and seeking to resolve misunderstandings?

Communication is a Two-Way Street

A leader's role includes being clear in their message. Clarity also requires feedback and confirmation from the message recipient. Insisting you stay on a one-way thoroughfare of dialogue will eventually lead you in the wrong direction and cause a wreck and here's why. What is clear to you may not be clear at all to someone else. Okay, I know that is a shock. Would you believe that even when something is clear in your own mind, that your mouth can betray you and muddle the entire message upon delivery? Ever said some- thing and then thought, "Where did that come from?""

It can be useful to think of communication as a process of sending and receiving messages with meanings as the attachment. Not everyone opens attachments. Not everyone trusts attachments. Not everyone takes the time to realize there are attachments! The attachments, if you will, are what clarifies the message and gives more detail and without them, your meaning can get really get fouled up in translation. The key elements of this communication process are illustrated here:[23]

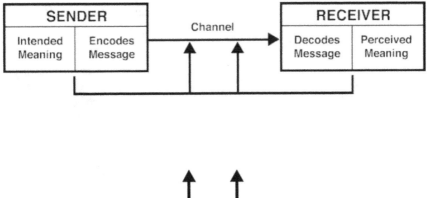

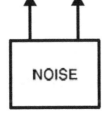

The elements of communication include a SOURCE, also known as a sender, who encodes the intended meaning into a message, and a RECEIVER, who decodes the message into a perceived meaning. (Look carefully and consider that phrase "perceived meaning") The receiver may or may not give feedback to the source. And although this process may appear to be very elementary, it is not quite as simple as it looks.[24]

If you are a driver, dominant, Commander, or red type of person, with a stereotypical Type A personality, speaking to an analytical Organizer or processor type of personality, you may not receive feedback because of intimidation factors or because they simply have not had enough time to process the appropriate feedback to be shared just yet. And, in the reverse, if you are an analytical, Organizer, processing type of person attempting to share your details with a specific structure, with a dominant or Commander-like character, you may find frustration in continually being cut off, interrupted and invited to get to the point faster. These are only two examples of the types of things that can slow down a message or mess up communication. Among other things, the elements that muddy the message, whether personality, preference, triggers, or an abundance of decibels, are called noise. Noise, quite simply, distorts understanding.

> **Noise is any disturbance that disrupts the message and interferes with the intended transfer of the message within the communication process.**

When we communicate, noise gets in our way. Besides the very obvious, such as our own thoughts, impatience, words, feelings, frustrations, pace, or volume, there are many types of noise. Noise is any disturbance that disrupts the message and interferes with the intended transfer of the message within the communication process. In addition, channels are the pathways through which messages are communicated.[25] I would even argue that your choice of channels could be your very own source of noise. Ever been the victim of a significant auto-correct error or included the kissy face emoji instead of the smiling emoji due to fat fingers?

Consider for a moment the statistic of word choice, tone of voice and body language. Regardless of the factual percentages, if most of one's message in the beginning of a conversation is sent with expressions and gestures, it could be said there's a lot of noise in email. Theoretically you're sending only a small portion of the entire meaning of the message and relying an awful lot on the interpretive skills (and mood!) of the recipient. Noise is present when the receiver inserts his or her own tone of voice into your words and assumes it is the same tone with which you sent the message. How many times could that possibly be a problem? We all do think the same, yes? (Sarcasm is hard to interpret in written text, given how much it is based on tone of voice, so let me help. INSERT SARCASM HERE.)

While we've listed many options, there are three primary types of noise that will halt traffic on the highway of communication. The first type is decibel noise, such as the annoying jack hammer outside your office window, or the lawn care team, who regularly seems to arrive at just the most important moment in most of my conversations.

Three Types of Noise Impacting Your Communication:

1. Decibel Noise – loud sounds, passing trucks, jack hammer

2. Psychological Noise – nagging feelings, insecurities, worry

3. Emotional Noise – significant trauma, loss, or grief consuming mindset

Noise types two and three are psychological noise and emotional noise. Just like the roar of a buzz saw, these are both increasingly difficult to tune out, especially the closer to home or closer to an emotional trigger, they become. Psychological noise would be the nagging feelings you arrive to the office with, after having had a heated morning argument with your parent or child or spouse. Emotional noise comes from more severe trauma and will prevent even the most adept listener from hearing your message. The brain only holds onto so much, and only has room for limited current pieces of information in the consciousness at one time. Those struggling with a long-term illness, loss of a loved one, or an event that consumes their mindset and emotions, are not hearing what you say with the same rational filter or clarity that might otherwise be an option.

Emotional and psychological issues tend to take up a lot of brain space and warp our perception of the world. What you thought was a very clear message may be interpreted differently at times of noise or fatigue. All the better reason to say what you mean and speak in clear terms, while also considering timing as a factor for noise reduction. Then clarify that what was clear to you was clear to your receiver.

Listening 101 was Not Offered in My School

Despite all the noise, you're currently reading this book, which means you're also probably saying the words silently to yourself. It's called sub vocalization. If you are moving your lips while reading, chances are good you're an extrovert and quite likely someone who learns better through physical movement. In all cases, you're reading a book I've written. Reading and writing are both forms of communication. So, are speaking and listening. In fact, those are considered to be the four main types of communication. How many hours a day do you spend doing one of or more of those simultaneously? The ability to do any one of them well is critical to your effectiveness as a leader and a person. Doing them simultaneously is a learned skill, and one at which most of us are not well skilled, but in today's workplace, doing just one is seen as slow and doing more than one at the same time is seen as essential for survival. The more you can communicate to the more people in the fastest time possible, the more you are seen as successful. Even Facebook has been found to give a badge of honor for speedy replies, the top tiers of which are within 15 minutes of receipt of any message, like, or comment.

> **The more you can communicate to the more people in the fastest time possible, the more you are seen as successful.**

One could actually argue that communication is the most important skill in life, not just leadership or in management. We spend most of our waking hours communicating one message or another. But consider this: You've spent years learning how to read, text, maybe write, and certainly type a message, years learning how to speak with words, from ABCs to from behind a lectern; but what about listening? Much conflict is brought on and continues when we have a culture of leaders who've only been taught to speak, but not to listen. What training or education have you had that enables you to muddle through the noise and the distractions and listen so that you really, deeply understand another human being from that individual's own frame of reference?[26]

Few people have had any training in listening at all. In fact, when I ask for a show of hands in my seminar of how many people have taken a public speaking class, most of the hands go up. When I ask the same question about a listening class, I see only two or three hands at most. Over the last few years this has increased slightly. I used to get strange looks at the question and no hands. Listening is a skill, not a technique, but a skill and a desire to really understand clearly what the other person is saying and meaning. If you want to interact effectively and communicate effectively with me, you must first understand me, as Stephen Covey points out in *The 7 Habits of Highly Effective People*. You must have the desire, and not try to use some fancy technique. As when I sense a technique, I may fear manipulation and thus be more afraid to be transparent and more vulnerable.to you, the listener. When fear and worry come into play in leadership, you begin to see events that include bottled feelings, followed by an explosive or volatile reaction, along with resentment and eventually expression that is far larger than the initial worry was in the first place. Learning to truly listen can proactively prevent gossip, drama, serious arguments and in some cases tragic circumstances.

What Does Clear Mean, Exactly?

I have a friend who virtually every time I ask if he understands what I mean of if I'm being clear, will say "Crystal". Somewhere along the way we have associated clarity with see through and that became the basis for the overuse of the word transparency in most organizations. As if clear means there is only one view and no other way to see the issue. Um, that would be a no.

Being clear simply means that the receiver heard the message in the same way that you intended. The receiver heard your intent, heard your words, heard your sincerity or lack of it, and heard your message in the way in which you intended. If you say to an employee that she is being reorganized, will she understand that you in fact mean her job no longer exists, or will she think you mean she is moving to another job or getting more responsibility? If you tell your boss that you would prefer to work with three other people, other than the one that he is recommending, does he understand that you are not willing to work with the person of his choice because of the person's work ethic, or does he think that you would rather work with your closest office friends or some other only known to you, interpretation? In the fast pace in which we all now live, spending more time on ensuring clarity so that your message recipient doesn't make an immediate, and off base assumption, is crucial. But, it also doesn't have to take a pain in the neck level of effort

We tend to play a game of assuming that the other person will understand our subtle, well-couched (means hidden between the cushions) message. The problem arises when she does not, and we blame her for not understanding what we said. In Corporate America, these assumptions are often fueled by the use and creation of fancy terminology, often for the purpose of sharing tough news in a way that is more delicate. But it's not just Corporate America, it's small businesses, government, education and

143

even in our home on TV and dinner table conversation. They're called buzz words. Ever used them? Use them long enough and they become normal. Use them long enough and you get to play a fun game of what I like to call Buzzword Bingo.

Buzzword Bingo!

The fun of Buzzword Bingo, also known as Lingo Bingo (a real game that exists and can be purchased), used to be that the boss was not in on the joke. Employees would make up game cards and slyly check the box with the appropriate word when the boss, leading the meeting, showed off his or her mastery of words that sounded impressive, but really meant nothing.[27]

As such, let it be said that using the following words DOES NOT MEAN you are speaking clearly. It may simply mean, that when it comes to Buzzword Bingo, you're helping a team member get closer to winning.

- Straw man

- Impact

- Corporate Synergy

- Reengineering

- Win-win

- Deep Dive

- Reorganizing

- Surplus

- Acquisition

- Core Competency

- Restructuring

- Out of the Box

- Empowerment

- Move the Needle

- Incentivize

- Leverage

- Strategic Planning/Thinking

- Innovation

- Ball Park

- Deliverable

- Drill down

- Legacy

- Mission Critical

- Harmonization

- Actualize

They all sound very important and meaningful, but do they mean anything really? Do they convey what one is really after or simply cause the leader to influence a group of head bobbing team members who appear to have gotten a clear message?

Buzzword Bingo began around the same time as the Dilbert cartoon, in the early 90's, and was initially a way for employees to get back at the big boss for being vacuous in an attempt to appear pompous. Some have even said that business people are always going to want to appear more pompous than they are by using such language. My question is would you prefer to be a business person, seen as pompous and special, or a leader others are willing and eager to follow? Hmmm?

When you want a team to modify their ability to work in harmony together, tell them how and about the four stages of team building. Avoid telling them to get more corporate synergy. When you tell those in your office you need a model of how the majority-favored solution would look in a variety of situations, give them the specifics, try not to send them on their way to create strawmen. When you want to define the ideal criteria for the ideal candidate for your open position, use plain English to describe behaviors and attributes and actions, instead of crafting each behavior trait into a properly worded, utterly meaningless core competency. Life is confusing enough without adding verbal interpretation of the language to the mix; speak to them clearly, specifically, and in a style perhaps even easily understood by their personality, which may be quite different from the style that comes to you most naturally.

Let's Get to the Bottom Line

So, that's the bottom line, is it not? Communicate clearly. Many managers and executives find that very phrase, the bottom line, to be another common, perfectly acceptable part of their vocabulary. However, now may be the time for you, as a leader, to realize that only twenty-five per cent of the population actually appreciates and understands the value of this phrase: the bottom line. There are hundreds of people out there roaming the planet who find this phrase ridiculous, overused, meaningless, and even offensive in light of the fact that so many details have been left out, at the time that phrase is used.

Are you someone who uses and believes in the value and virtue of this phrase? If so, you may wish to check with those employees that you have surrounded yourself with and see if they agree. If they do not, you are speaking to them in a language, or communication style, that they do not understand or appreciate. There are drivers and dominants, Commanders, Relaters and socializers, thinkers, analyticals, and Organizers, phlegmatics, melancholies, blues, reds, greens, yellows, and Entertainers out there. Whatever you choose to call someone's preference, be aware that their differences will show up in your communication and certainly will show up and be emphasized in theirs.

If you are talking with a direct, choleric, or Commander type of employee, use short sentences, stick to the facts and offer solutions that are black and white. If you find yourself speaking to a sanguine, or more social oriented Entertainer-type person, avoid critical words, emphasize her contributions and value and offer to let her call a friend. Do this, that is, if you wish to clearly communicate and have her understand your intent, while also being open to hearing the rest of your message. If you have no concern about whether or not she actually understands your message clearly, then I have two other suggestions: save your breath or prepare for miscommunication.

These are merely general communication and personality type guidelines and do not begin to touch on all the scenarios and personalities you may encounter. For more guidance on determining personalities and communicating uniquely with each of them, there are a number of resources out there. Florence Littauer was one of the front runners of her time on what she calls the four temperaments and described them clearly in her best-selling book *Personality Plus*. Dr. Tony Alessandra has authored a series called *Relationship Strategies*. In his works, I have found practical examples for reading others' communication style fairly quickly. He also gives suggestions for the questions to ask that will lead to a successful interpretation. There is also Dr. Sherry Buffington who, in partnership with her daughter Gina Morgan, developed the CORE Multi-Dimensional Awareness Profile (MAP) Assessment® and wrote the book *Who's Got the Compass? I Think I'm Lost*. The CORE MAP® Profile is the one we have used in our development of leaders for the last fifteen years.

I encourage you to review, listen to, or even indulge in the experience of each of these books and assessment tools, in order to gain a better understanding of just how unique each employee really is, including you.

You Look Upset.. You okay?

We put forth the effort to understand our friends, but at work it seems to be different. Though our friends are also often those with whom we already have a certain number of things in common in communication and many other areas. In fact, we might say this to a friend, "You look upset. You okay?". Would we always say it to an employee, much less a boss, or

> **Remember to remain aware that there are people out there who are happy people who simply forgot to tell that to their face.**

do we simply assume we understand what's going on based on that facial expression or body stance. When setting the example for employees' morale or enthusiasm, check your own messages first. Then confirm the message that you see from others, with questions. This does not mean you must follow everyone around the office constantly asking them what this means or that means. It does mean that you cease and desist assuming that someone's crossed or folded arms means that they're closed off or resistant, and you should assume they're disinterested in the job. It does mean that you realize there are people out there, who may work with you, who are tremendously happy people, who simply forgot to tell their face. Are you one of those? Do you ever become focused and forget to take notice of the expression on your face?

In a seminar I taught on customer service, I was asked by a participant what to do if the boss did not LIKE any of his employees. Those were her words, and I followed them up with a series of questions. Does he smile a lot? Does he talk to people in the office? Does he require near-perfect quality work? Is he consistently talking about the point, the bottom line and the results? Does he come in early and stay late? She answered no to the first two and yes to all of rest and was surprised that I had described him so accurately.

She was a social type of person who cherished interaction and emotions and time with people, and he was a driver who almost struggled to spell emotions, much less feel them or show them, but could spell perfectionism in his sleep without a pen. I doubt seriously he realized the effect he was having on the morale level in the office (she was apparently not the only one who felt this way). The employees assumed they knew how he felt and fed off of it, reacting to him as if that was without question, how he felt. I wonder if they ever spoke about it. I wonder if your assumptions will now become those "truths" that you question.

Miscommunications abound in situations in which there are multiple cultures, multiple beliefs, multiple ages, races, colors, and so on. A simple nod from a man can confuse a woman, as he means yes. She will, however, probably say something like "Are you sure?" knowing that a woman's nod only means acknowledgement, which is a far cry from yes. When we hear these things in a comedy skit we laugh because they are true and quite funny, when we're not in the middle of interpreting them. When we hear such truths at the office, the wrong interpretation is far less funny and can cause an employee or leader to be labeled for the length of his career.

Eye contact, invasion of personal space, positioning of office furniture, open or closed doors, and a firm grip or clammy fish handshake, all have an impact on the message you send. If you say one thing with your words, yet do something different with your body, tone or even office furniture, you will confuse those you are trying to address. If your mantra is that you have an open-door policy, and yet you arrange your office so that there is a clear barrier between you and whoever has passed through the door, something does not match. If you say you're a leader, even make it known that you are seeking a higher-level position or promotion but have a handshake that feels like your wrist has lost all muscle, it's a mismatch and a problem. People typically believe what they see and experience far more than what they heard. If you severely chastise those who gossip and perpetuate the rumor mill, and yet you are the first to share with the team every leaked detail from your "friend" on the board of directors, the experience and your words don't line up.

How many of those scenarios are you creating in your office? Leaders walk their talk and have matching messages in both word and deed. Think of the colleague of yours who bugs you because of a cross look she gave you six months ago, that the two of you have never bothered to discuss. Setting the example does not limit itself to rolling up your sleeves to do the work; it also includes demonstrating how and in what manner you would like to see work get done.

Know and trust that your words, body language, tone, actions, and behaviors are continually evaluated and possibly emulated by those who want to achieve the level you have. Managers send mixed messages. Leaders show and provide clear communication.

Learn, Lead, and Then Listen

Leaders listen; most managers wait to make a response. The best communicators realize that a person has two ears and one mouth for a reason. That ratio should mean that we utilize the ears twice as much as the mouth. I personally think some people have those backwards, as they seem to talk incessantly without really listening to the responses, or they talk to themselves while someone else is talking so that the perfect response is already crafted and ready the moment the person stops speaking.

You can continue to do that, but I promise you will miss most of the message that the sender is trying to give you. Just as we can speak clearly and set the example, there are ways to listen better and more effectively; the point of both is to have a productive and effective transference of the message from the sender to the receiver, whomever he or she may be.

In order to facilitate effective listening, the following are ten helpful guidelines to follow.

Ten Listening Guidelines for Leaders:

1. Listen to the Words the Person Uses

2. Listen for Communication Style

3. Note General Personality and Mood

4. Observe Body Language

5. Mirror Body Language

6. Make Eye Contact

7. Focus on Keeping your Mind Present

8. Avoid as Much Noise as Possible

9. Take a Breath Before Speaking

10. Consider Your Words Before Using Them

Listen to the Words the Person Uses

Listening is a skill that can, could, and often should, be improved. Though word choice does only account for a small portion of the meaning of most messages you receive, it is the foundation many times for what someone is trying to say. Hearing only the words will not get you complete clarity but hearing everything except for the words will leave you without some necessary details.

Listen for Communication Style

The communication style you use may or may not be the same as your audience. As much of a shocker as that often is, I felt it warranted repeating. Your goal is to make your communication as much like your audience's as possible. This is not about mocking your audience or your receiver; it is about effectively communicating with them, so they feel understood.

Communication styles are comprised of things like use of vocabulary, accent, and tone of voice, pace of delivery, facial expressions and body language. This is not an all-inclusive list, but a sampling of what you should be looking for. Does the person have an advanced vocabulary, and does she choose her words carefully? Does he take time to listen to your words or the words of others speaking, and then pause before contributing? A person who processes information before speaking communicates very differently from someone who speaks immediately upon hearing silence.

Note General Personality and Mood

This type of observation does not require a psychology degree, but rather a mere interest in paying attention. If the sender of your message is dealing with several emotional issues outside of the office, or just got off the phone with an irate caller, his words to you may be the same as usual, but his tone may differ drastically. Even the happiest of more dominant personalities will communicate differently from an analytical thinker on his best day.

If you ignore the differences in those around you and expect them to be all just like you and communicate just like you, your life will be continually frustrating, and people will start to get tired of what you keep expecting. Not to mention the fact that the world would become a very boring place if everyone said the same thing in the same manner.

Observe Body Language

Crossed or folded arms…go ahead, tell me what that means. Better yet, find a group of people and ask them all what it means and tell me how many different answers you get. Body language, depending on the gender, culture, and age of a person, means different things to different people. Do not make the mistake of insisting one gesture means one thing. Instead, simply observe the person you are talking with and take in all their gestures. Interpretations are much more accurate when made from a cluster of gestures, or the big picture.

Someone with folded arms, crossed legs, and shivering, might be cold. Someone with crossed legs, folded arms, a pursed lip expression, turned up nose, and body turned slightly away from you, might be closed to hearing anything else you have to say. See how easy that is? Pay attention to all of it, instead of just a piece of the puzzle. How many intricate landscapes are you aware of that fit onto one puzzle piece?

Mirror Body Language

Be clear that mirror and mock are two different things. What I have found occurs naturally between two people having a conversation is that they will slowly come to hold the same body position. If one is crossing legs, the other will eventually do the same. If one has their hand resting under the chin comfortably, the other will follow suit.

If you wish to increase the level of comfort another person feels around you, simply, SLOWLY, convert your body language to mirror that of him or her. This is not the same as copying his or her every movement, as you can imagine how annoying or creepy that would be. I think you get the idea.

Make Eye Contact

If you are in a country doing business where eye contact is as highly prized as it is in America, then do as the Romans do and make eye contact often and with many. If you are outside of America or in a country that does not emphasize or appreciate and evaluate eye contact, exercise caution, as there are reasons in diverse cultures for not making eye contact, depending on your gender and other factors.

In the United States, the typical response when asked how people feel if someone does not make eye contact, it is that he or she must be up to something or is somehow shady or shy. Be aware that if you do not look someone in the eye, chances are he will create questions that lead to not possibly respecting you or she will think you have low self-esteem. Either can be detrimental to your conversation and the perceptions that follow.

Focus on Keeping your Mind Present

Did you know that the average attention span of an adult is about the same as that of a young child? It falls somewhere between eight and thirteen minutes, about the amount of time between commercials on a TV program. However, recent studies liken attention span to that of a gold fish, which is apparently closer to 8 SECONDS, though it is unclear how the attention span of a goldfish might be measured. Regardless, if you consider how much information we take in and are bombarded with regularly, it is no wonder we have difficulty paying attention to just one little conversation at a time.

Effective listeners focus on the sender and keep themselves checked in to the conversation. No grocery list making while someone else is talking.

Shush the internal dialogue. I have found that asking questions, making eye contact, and repeating their words in my head, are most helpful strategies when I am trying to focus. In fact, if I am trying to listen carefully and focus on a phone call, I will often don the headset and look at the phone itself to help me remember that there is someone else on the other end.

Avoid as Much Noise as Possible

"Huh? Can you hear me? Hang on. Wait until this truck passes." Highway driving and talking is efficient and falls in the category of multi-tasking. It is way of life for most of us and a way to make reasonably good use of time that would otherwise be spent solely focused on traffic or music. The noise factor, however, is a challenge and something to be aware of when talking. If you can avoid the noise factor in many of your conversations, you will have more productive and clear message transfers. Noise is anything that keeps you from hearing the sender's message and one could argue the mere act of driving, which requires your attention, provides noise to any conversation since you're spending a large portion of your talking and listening time paying attention to the road, or at least that's what is supposed to be happening.

Avoid serious conversations at the office when your mind is elsewhere, or at least alert people that your mind is elsewhere so that they can try to change sending channels. When I am traveling and am only able to speak with loved ones by phone or email, the guideline we've have made is to reserve serious "This is how I feel and I am upset" types of conversation for when I return home, so that I am able to fully listen to the entire message, without noise and with the other added benefit of body language for interpretation. Even Facetime doesn't give you the entire picture.

Take a Breath Before Speaking

Few people like to be interrupted, but I think even fewer appreciate the opportunity to repeat themselves because you didn't hear them the first time. A sure sign of an ineffective listener is that person who is actively listening until you say something with which she is in disagreement. She then immediately begins to jump into the conversation.

Out of respect, she lets you finish, but she has not heard a word you said after the point that caught her attention or tripped her trigger. These types of listeners formulate the response that they wish to give while you are still talking and immediately begin to speak when you take a breath. A better listening activity is to focus on what the other person is saying until he finishes, and then take a breath before speaking, allowing yourself time to gather your thoughts. With Chatty Cathy, you may find it takes a while to get your thoughts out or point across, but if she really feels heard, chances are she will reduce the chatty behavior. Most people talk so much more because, so few people actually listen at the level that makes them feel heard. (That and we think far faster than we speak)

Consider Your Words Before Using Them

If your audience speaks quickly, so should you in your delivery. If your audience speaks slowly, use caution in your delivery so as not to offend or give your listener the impression that you are mimicking her with ill will or condescension.

The same is true for accents. Unless you have established a strong rapport with your audience already, reproducing their accent in your delivery may prove offensive, and quickly. The issue of an accent is about awareness and possible presence of communication barriers.

Use of similar pace and tone, unless you are speaking to someone who is verbally disabled, is a sign that you listened to the sender's style closely. You want to respond in a way that you know works for him or her, as opposed to the only style you thought you knew up to this point: your own. In the case of someone who is unable to speak clearly due to injury or illness, listen carefully, but do not take on stylistic differences such as a stutter, slur, lisp, or any other traits that could be seen as mockery. In all cases, common sense and empathy are good accompaniments to listening.

Listen up!

In a world in which most of us multi-task our way through the day and leave the television on for noise, constantly stare at our phone and videos, dinging noises, texts and messages, listening gets lost between the drive-through and the commercials. For our purposes, listening actively would include acknowledging the other's contribution and clearing your mind of other distractions and potential responses. In short, hearing, listening, and focus. You must focus, grasshopper, focus.

You must also find ways to say what you mean in clear, plain language and vocabulary so that all those around you understand your message. If you choose not to change your style, you want to instead, make it clear to those around you that you encourage clarifying questions. If you require that all understand your communication style, as if it is the only one out there, you may be in for a big shock, along with the realization that you are dead wrong and often misunderstood or at some point, ignored because trying to understand is too hard.

It is simply amazing that with over four billion people on the planet, with dozens of different communication styles, hundreds of thousands of behaviors, and over six thousand different spoken languages, any one of us can ever actually understand a single, tiny piece of transmission from any single other person on the planet. If you wish to lead, you must learn to bridge the gap with at least those you lead. Speak to them clearly, according to them, and demonstrate what you are asking them to do, so that they see what you say, and then stop talking, and listen.

Once they are done listening and hopefully take a breath, stand back and be prepared, because if you have asked them to listen very carefully, they may have formed an opinion, and once they have listened to you, they...

...might actually tell you their opinion.

8 LEADERS REMAIN OPEN TO THE OPINIONS OF OTHERS

There's more than one way to skin a cat," say my friends from Texas. And oddly enough, there's more than one way to do just about anything. There's more than one way to create a budget report, more than one way to file client records, more than one way to develop a presentation for the biggest client, and certainly more than one way to build rapport with others.

The latter was added to that list because it seems easier to see; everyone has his or her own style in making relationships and connecting. Many managers are driven, focused individuals with a wild idea that the way they want to do it is truly the only way to do whatever IT is. Leaders however, look upon each incident, project, event, and follower, as an individual or specific occurrence, and take in a wide array of options and inputs before making a definitive decision. Much, and in fact most, of these inputs and options can come from those you have the privilege of leading

The Turnip Truck Did Not Bring These People

Those who work with you did not reside next to the soft, fluffy moss under a river rock for the years of their life that inched by until the moment they encountered you and you became their boss. In fact, I bet they had a life, or at least some semblance of one. That life has been filled with enriching, learning, and even difficult experiences that you may be able to avoid personally living through if you will only allow for the value of their viewpoint. Remember the difference between experience and wisdom?

Allow for employee opinions even and especially when they differ from your own. You may be surprised by the wisdom they possess. The truth is, we as humans tend to believe that our perspective, our beliefs, and our perceptions, are spot-on accurate without doubt and rarely do we argue with our own data. I did say "tend to," as there are many thinkers out there who allow for other pieces of information to float in and modify their initial thought or belief. However, most of us see things the way that we believe they should be seen.

The way we see things is called perspective and much like in the movie Vantage Point, it all depends on the angle from which one is looking. Perspective develops from the time we are about six until the ripe old current age of now. Once developed, we operate on the assumption that this perception is correct, and still current, more as a comfortable habit or survival skill than some pompous assumption.

How would we survive if we were unsure about everything and had to pause for analysis before making a single move in any direction? Ever watched the animated sloth move in a Disney movie? The trouble with these perceptions is if we believe they are right, then that leaves little room for the possibility that others' perceptions, perhaps differing greatly from our own, may also be valid. Those other people's perceptions developed just as long ago as ours did and sometimes even long before ours were formed. It is not as if their perceptions came with the "some assembly required" stamp affixed to their box that the turnip truck dropped off yesterday. Neither did you recently install the software that allowed you to view their perceptions, when you hired or inherited these employees. They are a phone that already came with a number of apps to be used. Nothing needs to be done other than asking them for the information. Think about that for a moment.

What You Think About is What You Become

Managers are often unaware of the nonverbal impact they have on the thoughts and opinions of other employees. For that matter, managers and people are often unaware of the impact they have when they fail to control the voices in their own head. Thankfully, over the last decade that does appear to be changing in some areas. What you think about is, in fact, what you become, and that has been a lesson we've heard from Socrates, Hippocrates, Epictetus, Ben Franklin, Napoleon Hill, Joe Karbo, and many others, long before it became a mainstream "secret" that just now was able to be revealed. The first time I heard this statement, was from leadership guru and internationally acclaimed author and speaker, Brian Tracy.

For a moment, think of something you are really passionate about, and then try to describe it to a close friend of yours with an Eeyore-like, pessimistic and down type of tone. It will be fairly obvious you're being fake in your down demeanor and before long you may both end up laughing. They won't buy it or believe your attempt and will probably ask you to quit pulling their leg. People can tell when you are thinking something other than what you articulate. We now call it being fake, but it's so much bigger than that and easier to detect than you might think. This is why you only ask for opinions and express concern if you want them and have some.

> **People can tell when you are thinking something other than what you articulate.**

Like it or not, there can be no contact between an employee and a manager or leader that does not result in the communication of a feeling, attitude, or belief system. Your facial expression, a part of that sixty- four per cent of the interpretation we attributed to body language, including how you walk, how and where you sit in a meeting, and what you wear—all serve to (define and reveal) your attitude, especially if it's a bad one.[28]

A bad attitude is the worst thing that can happen to a group of people, and one of the symptoms of a bad attitude or extreme negativity is the closing out of other people's inputs or opinions. The worst of all scenarios is if this attitude is attached to the manager. Negative managers are like movie monsters whose personality and management style wrecks everything in their path throughout the entire department and create a sense of tension that keeps everyone on the edge of their seat looking for the super hero to arrive and frustrated when that doesn't happen.

When you talk about managers (Note that leaders are rarely called leaders if they possess a bad attitude) with a negative attitude, the illustration of a monster is probably close to most people's perceptions. And a monster can be one who is negative about people's uniqueness, people's need to grow, their need not to be micromanaged, their need to be allowed to share input. This lack of input allowance is one of the easiest symptoms to spot. The reality is that most managers display this negative behavior overtly, whereas the others affected by a negative attitude often give much more subtle signals. No matter what your level, your comfort with others' needs or opinions, or the level of the employees that you have the privilege of managing, each person has valid opinions and a need, and right, to share them. Out of respect, courtesy, civility, and a need for input and creativity other than our own, we, as leaders, should stop, listen, validate, and accept those opinions.

R-E-S-P-E-C-T

People want to feel a part of the big picture. You can no longer afford to treat employees in the old-world fashion of top- down dictatorship, which is common among new, young, and perhaps inexperienced managers. Even without a financial interest in the business, employees want to be considered "partners" or at least those who are valued and will even demand such respect—and rightfully so, in my opinion. The loosening-up of the hierarchical and stuffy "brass" in major corporations over the last twenty years reflects this need for employees to feel at least as important as the boss.[29] Though this can be expressed in a number of ways, one was is to say that employees need to know that the manager, boss, and in this case, the leader, values each individual employee and respects the opinions of each. Even more importantly, leaders are human and approachable and demonstrate to others who choose to follow them, that people are people, and we all put our pants on in the same way.

Adults like to make their own choices about their own destiny. If they have chosen to be led by you, do not take away their influence over their own future by disallowing their opinion. Adults like to be in control of themselves; allowing for their opinion and using their input, or at the very least validating their input by listening, gives them the chance to be heard and to know that they have done their best to control their environment.

This really is all about respect. When you care enough to ask, it helps if you care enough to listen, and if you care enough to listen, it helps if you care enough to validate. Should you find that you don't care and do not respect, you may have no business asking, as you will not listen, and as such, you will have difficulty validating. In this case, you might want to reconsider the role of leading. If, instead, you allow for other people's opinions, even when they differ from your own, you show them one of the greatest forms of respect.

A Word on Respect

Should you find that you don't care about those you lead, you may have no business asking them for anything other than the bare minimum. Anything else you should ask for, you'll not be willing to listen to their input or suggestions and as such will be unable to validate what you're thinking or feeling. Given the crucial role of respect in the feedback loop and communication, much less collaborative efforts, should you find you lack some, you may wish to reconsider the role of leading. Respect is one of those elements that if you weren't taught it at a young age, you would be well served to conjure it, muster it, or practice it before accepting a promotion.

So, What's the Point?

You are the boss and you have final say-so, right? Well, only if you want to lead a team of one. You may have final authority and be able to make the final decision, but if you do it in a vacuum, soon you will be sucking up the blame for leaving everyone else out. You'll be seen an unapproachable and not a team player. Start shifting your mindset to reflect a belief that others' opinions have great value. New employees have new ideas from other places. New workers, fresh from college, have a new perspective from an untarnished viewpoint. Even children, fairly new to the world, have a fresh perspective that we are consistently amazed by and by which we're frequently entertained. Of course, we are not managing children when at the office. We do not lead children, or even people who act like them, though it may at times feel that way and be even easier to say. Exercise caution in this case.

Adults often exhibit traits similar to that of children, such as the same attention spans or tantrums; we just tend to hide it better. One thing, however, that adults lose, that children are famous for, is unmitigated daring and lack of fear. Children will try anything, even when told "no" a hundred times. Adults expect "no" before you say it and will shy away from sharing ideas or opinions because of their own self-esteem, or lack thereof, as well as from fear of being struck down, made to look stupid, or possibly even of succeeding.

The first reason you allow for others' opinions is out of respect; the second is out of courtesy and a clear display that you are not the only one whose opinion counts; the third may be because others may know more than you. Really! (Breathe deeply…) An additional reason to allow for and encourage input from others you lead, even if the input is vastly different from your own, is the fact that without involvement, there is no commitment. Let me repeat. Without involvement, there is no commitment. No matter how compelling your argument or persuasion for buy-in and involvement and engagement, no involvement means no commitment.

> **Without involvement,
> there is no commitment.**

When a person is new to an organization, you can essentially give him a goal and he will accept it, particularly if the orientation for new employees

4 Reasons to Remain Open to the Opinions of Others:

1. It is a sign of respect.

2. It shows professionalism, courtesy, and value of another.

3. It allows others with more expertise to shine and contribute.

4. It increases buy-in and engagement from team members.

and the training share these expectations. But as people become more mature and their own lives take on a deeper meaning, they want involvement and significant involvement. If they do not get involvement, they do not buy into whatever you or your organization is selling. At that point, you then have a significant motivational challenge which cannot be overcome at the same level of thinking that created it.[30]

Make things a little easier on yourself and certainly more effective for the group you wish to lead; give them that chance to buy into and contribute to what you are working on when it affects them. If you do, you will find much less need for directing, controlling, criticizing, or commanding the team will have bought into the core of the issue and be self-motivated to work with what they have suggested.

Can I Clone You?

His name was Paul and he was a small, grandfatherly type figure with a Santa Claus demeanor, button nose, and jovial nature. He laughed easily and looked at me rather strangely when I began making requests for him to organize workbooks and handouts for the seminar I was to conduct in an hour.

Paul was what's called the program manager for a public seminar, and had I stopped my fretting and looked around long enough, I would have noticed that Paul had already sorted workbooks, stacked hand- outs, and organized the registration process in a way that I had never seen or thought of before this session. His strange look, I later discovered, was due to his uncertainty about my approval of the way he had put things together. I am sure he was waiting for approval or to be told it was all wrong by some speaker with a super-human ego and he did later reveal that he'd been fussed for his initiative a time or two.

Add to that, I'm normally a bit of a control freak in this area, or as I call it a *recovering control freak who regularly forgets the steps.* Normally, I would have taken two seconds to look at his way and dismiss it as not possibly as efficient as the way I would have done it. Not my way equates to wrong. A hard sentence to write, even as I'm typing, given how far from the truth it is and yet how powerful a belief it is for most. However, this time I was in a hurry, running late, exhausted after sixteen straight days of conducting public seminars in sixteen different cities, and too tired to redo all of his efforts with grace and finesse. So, this time I decided to "make do" with someone else's method. Well, that was the last time I ever even considered any method OTHER THAN Paul's and that, is perhaps the biggest lesson.

He had taken the workbooks and sorted them into stacks of ten, so that he could count at a glance the number of participants in the classroom. He had a basket of pens from the hotel set up at the end of the registration table, so that learners could sign their admission ticket while waiting in line, instead of holding up the line while he searched for their name on the roster and someone else used the one pen that I always made available. He had taped workbooks to the doorway of our classroom and the registration table, so that all eighty-seven learners were clear about which table in the hall was theirs and which room in the hallway was the one they were to find a seat in which to sit.

You see, I had been conducting seminars for this company for about nine months. Paul had been acting as a temporary program manager for this company for about nine years and had previously owned his own seminar company in which he put on large-scale seminars. I had approached each program manager for previous sessions as if I was his or her manager and most of the time, he or she had not done this type of work before. Thus, I would usually have to teach them quickly and do most of the work myself. I had a system that I had always used and that worked. Why fix things if they aren't broken, right?

That day, I learned a valuable leadership lesson. Paul reminded me that others' ideas and input can spur creativity that you would otherwise miss if you continued to do things in the same manner repeatedly. If you truly want to tap into that resource of both new and long-time employees, the show of respect, the civility in asking for their opinion, and that possible fountain of creativity, should be incentive enough. Yet, one more thing is a must. You must make the environment conducive to conflict-free discussion. This includes an open and encouraging sharing of ideas with zero fear of rejection on the part of the employee. Sounds simple, right?

How Do I Do That?

There is a saying that goes like this: "If you don't care, don't ask and if you don't have any concern, don't try to express any." You may recall my saying that once or twice already. One of the key elements to creating an encouraging and open environment in which people will honestly share their opinions, is authenticity, also known as sincerity. If you are truly interested in the opinions of others and are convinced, as a result of this reading, or perhaps based on other readings and experiences, that this is the way to go, your sincerity will show through in the way that you express your interest. Make your intentions clear before you ask for feedback, particularly if you're dealing with veteran employees or baby boomers and this is not the experienced they have been used to with previous managers or leaders.

As a fairly new leader, I inherited a staff of seven employees in a department store area. The area that I managed had been previously managed by a manager who'd been there since the invention of the wheel and had a reputation for subscribing to the "My way or the highway" school of management. The departure of this manager was followed by months of no supervision, which led to a group of very independent sales people who believed they were an effective self-directed team who no longer needed a manager. Period. And then I came along. I was a young whipper-snapper with a theory about how things were supposed to work, who was ready to put them to work and have them utilize all of my age-old wisdom. I was in my early 20's. Stop laughing at me. Or if you *are* in your early 20's, please know the term age-old wisdom was laced with sarcasm. My first attempts at opening up dialogue and asking for feedback backfired, as the employees saw me as weak and lacking in credibility. However, I continued to ask, as I felt it important for them to understand that I valued their opinion. They had been there longer, and I wanted their input, as they were closer to many of the problems the department faced than I ever would be as a newer manager.

I shared with a couple of the employees the reasons why I was asking and what I was looking to accomplish in gaining their feedback. Slowly, they seemed to come around and share, but it was a slow process. Then a few others learned from the other employees that I really did seem to care (and in fact, I did!) about their opinion and in many small ways was acting on the input I received from them. Finally, after about a month, there were several examples of how I had solicited an opinion, taken it into consideration, and then given credit to the employee who had the idea, if it went well and was what we needed as a department. The long-term employees then began to speak out.

Step one is to have patience. Step two involves explaining your intentions and what you would like to do with the input you are seeking. Mind you, there will be times when you cannot use the input you get, for several possible reasons. The important thing to remember is that you do not dismiss the input simply because you cannot use it at that moment or in that instance. Step three simply involves doing what you say you are going to do. But before any of those steps, you must first care. Don't try to fake it and act as if. The results will be different if you are truly not interested in the input for which you've asked. The final and most effective step in encouraging honest input and open dialogue is to actually do something with the input you get. Even the smallest of efforts or actions displays you were able to give an employee credit for input or put into action an idea that an employee gave you will do amazing things to boost morale and show others that you mean business when you ask for input.

4 Steps for Soliciting Input:

1. Ask questions authentic interest and patience.

2. Explain your intentions.

3. Set the example.

4. Use the input you've been given and act on what you can.

This is not to say that you are going to ask for employee opinions, listen to all those that differ from yours and encourage disagreement, while then going along with the most disagreeable idea and setting the employee up for failure with your boss. This also does not imply that you are going to ask for input and act on it in any way if it is detrimental, or not in the best interest of the company or the business or the group that you manage. And of course, if you are lacking in creative methods to ask for feedback, you may always use the ever-popular suggestion box, survey method, comment cards, or just plain old asking. The key to remember is to avoid asking unless you care, and that an opinion different from yours or upper management's is not wrong, but DIFFERENT!

How Can You Think That?

Deeply held and long trusted beliefs may trip you up when you receive input. You may find that you have a deeply seated belief that states, "If you say you will be on time, then you arrive on time." Or do you find that whenever you get there is the time that you should have arrived? Whether you are on one side or the other, you are correct, according to your belief system. Belief systems are what guide our ideas of correct and incorrect, accurate and inaccurate, and what we use to judge others. If you believe you, and everyone else, should always be on time, then those who are not on time may elicit feelings from you that sound like "What is wrong with you people?!" when in fact, nothing is wrong. They simply have a different belief system. But the decision that they're doing it wrong happens very quickly so stay on top of it so that you avoid labeling someone as difficult, who is merely fond of believing differently.

When others have different opinions, different beliefs, and different perspectives, we tend to see them as not only different, but wrong. The unfortunate truth is that we tend to discredit those ideas, concepts, truths, and opinions that do not align with our own personal belief systems. Think of the belief you have about how you are supposed to look in the morning before you leave the house. If you do not match that image, how hard is it for you to accept a compliment that day on how good you look? Do you really accept it and revel in the delight of being complimented, or do you brush it off as something that person said just to be nice? In asking for input from others and allowing for those you manage to have individual opinions and beliefs and perspectives, you are respecting the individuality that is already present in every person. Denying it and trying to create conformity can be dangerous. Embrace the different viewpoint and allow for it, even when it differs from your own. The world would be mighty boring if we all thought, viewed, perceived, and believed in the same manner. In fact, if you've not already seen it, now would be a good time to Google and review or share the TEDx talk of *When Did We All Become Difficult People?*

On that note of everyone being the same being boring, the team I managed for a wireless company was anything but boring. They taught me a great deal and, most importantly, gave me their opinions. I managed a team of fourteen trainers who worked in five states and had customers in over five different call centers, taking calls from more than eleven different markets. What an incredible hotbed for possible communication errors! One year I brought them all into Orlando for a team meeting over the holiday season. It was the first time many of them had met each other in person, as with our geography, conference calls and video chats or texts were the medium of choice for meetings.

When I brought them all together and reinforced that this meeting was for them and I was in need of their input, it was a wonderful experience. They talked during the meeting, outside of the meeting, when we went to dinner, with me, with others, amongst themselves and even with a few of the employees at the hotel who happened to pop in to refresh our break, about our challenges and how we could solve them. On the second day of the meeting, after a few pre-planned presentations by their peers, I asked each person to record on flip charts what they thought the challenges were that stood in the way of meeting our team objectives and goals. We then, as a group, came up with pages of solutions for each problem and a few new goals on which everyone was now eager to get started.

From that point on, there was no need for me to remind team members of action items or to keep track of how we were progressing, except for performance reviews and record-keeping. Because the team members had come up with their own solutions to their own problems, they managed themselves and were intrinsically driven to see their ideas come to life and stay alive. We built programs out of that meeting that lasted for over a year, even into a time in the company when morale reached an all-time low point. That team learned skills that they still use today, and I learned the power of asking for input, a skill that I use daily. The bond and camaraderie we experienced out of sharing ideas and input is one that I encourage you to try to experience and duplicate.

What If It Gets Out of Hand?

There are some exceptions to the value of input from all team members. No one is perfect. Some opinions that you are soliciting may cause a conflict or two in your group, team or department. Conflict is good, as long as you see it for what it is and don't let it become the focus. A conflict is merely a point at which two things are at odds, or opposing, or in contradiction to one another. Well, good gracious, unless you live in perpetual fairytale where everything happens perfect and there's never any accidents, un-ohs, opinions, or foibles, you will at some point encounter conflict. It is not all bad and awful and negative, as confrontation is not all bad, awful and negative. It simply means you disagree on a point and then are at liberty to agree to disagree and move on. It is when both parties are incapable of doing this that things become a bit of a challenge.

Asking for and allowing for the opinions of others, including those you manage, does not mean that you exonerate yourself from decision making authority. You are not giving this up; you are merely allowing more input to be a part of your decision. Often a negative conflict can arise if those whose opinion you seek believe that opinions mean decision-making authority. To avoid this type of conflict, make your intentions clear early on. Asking for the opinions of others, including those you manage, does not mean that you will take what he or she says as the gospel truth and act on it solely and immediately. Can we say reality check? You must be cautious and clear in making known your intended use for such information and opinions.

Asking for the opinions of others, including those you manage, can mean that you ask for the opinions and then agree to disagree. It can also mean that you ask for the opinions and then respond to questions that require you to validate your own opinions. It can also mean that the bottom line remains unchanged, but that the way it is approached, or delivered, or communicated, is modified slightly because of the input and opinions you received.

Once You Ask For it, Can You Take It?

I suppose that section title could be seen as a dare or challenge, much like telling a five-year-old she can't watch the entire movie of Frozen before falling asleep while singing. However, you see it, can you take it? Can you endure the effort to reap the reward of those efforts? Can you watch the entire movie without sleeping when you're five and exhausted? The answer to all question is another one: How bad do you want it? Each of these ways of asking for others' opinions requires a manager or leader to be secure in his or her own opinions and beliefs and interested in engaging team members.

How secure are you, and what are you doing to encourage the opinion-sharing of those who report to you? What will you do when those opinions are slightly or vastly different from your own opinions? Will you tell the employee that you disagree? Will you try to keep his or her self-esteem intact? Will you try to shelter his or her feelings while temporarily stifling his or her growth? Whatever you decide to do, your behavior and words are considered to be something you're dishing out and if you dish out something out, be sure that you can take what you might get back. Keep in mind that if you are asking for input and allowing for others' opinions, you are dishing out some additional responsibility to these folks. You are asking them to think for themselves and then articulate those thoughts. What you may also dish out is feedback on how or whether their input can be put to good use addressing the current issue.

If you cannot take what you dish out, so to speak, or take similar feedback from those you wish to lead and handle their new-found sense of ownership and interest and engagement, then perhaps it is best that you forget about feedback and opinion solicitation. If, on the other hand, you put to use the first eight steps to becoming a better leader and transition from mere manager, you will have some very confident, talented, and creative employees and followers who want you to grow just as much as you have wanted growth for them. Part of the growing is learning to take feedback...

...even from those you are managing to lead even better.

9 LEADERS GIVE HONEST FEEDBACK

Over the years, I have taught more than five hundred classes on How to Overcome Negativity in the Workplace. In each course, there has always been a section in which we discuss how to overcome someone else's perception that you might be the one who is negative. The first action item in this section is to ask for feedback from people who perceive you that way. Every time I get to this part I throw in a couple of extra pointers, such as: 1) Always choose your timing carefully; right after your boss chews you out is probably not the best time to ask him or her for feedback; 2) Always choose your audience carefully; the office gossip monger was probably not a wise feedback choice; and 3) Always tell the person you are asking what you will do with the feedback and why you are asking for his or her feedback.

The one thing that I have often failed to caution learners on is to beware and be prepared to take what one dishes out. When you are the one being asked to provide feedback, be kind. Sooner than you might like to think or anticipate, that same recipient might be in a position to be giving you some feedback. Most people will tell you that they would like to hear it "straight from the horse's mouth," or will tell you to "Give to me like it is," or command you to "Just tell me; I can take it." They no more mean that than they mean to drive their car off a bridge. Yet those of us who are direct, driven, focused, and in a leadership or managerial role fall for it every time. The efficiency of just being able to say what's on or mind without preamble or a filter gives in to our better judgment and we proceed to provide someone with the candid, direct feedback they asked for. Honest feedback does not always have to be hurtful or direct. It just has to be honest, and not everyone wants complete honesty, either.

Feedback is Not the Same as Criticism

We tend to look upon "feedback" as the buzzword for criticism. Then we add insult to injury and call that criticism, constructive. What is constructive about someone telling you their version of what they think you're doing wrong? Do most people do things wrong on purpose? Not usually. So, perhaps if we just call it feedback instead of criticism they will not catch on to the fact that you are criticizing the work they have done. You must be kidding?! This works in much the same way that the word surplus, as in your job has been surplussed, covers up job-loss. Maybe that should have been on the buzzword-bingo list in bold, as it is used far more often than is the truth. Feedback is just feedback. It is information, which is inherently neutral until subjected to someone's perception. It is just information—not good, not bad. Giving feedback is providing others with the development tool of a progress report. It is letting others know how they are doing against the clear expectations that have been set and hopefully shared. And as the old adage we used earlier says, it is in so many ways, not "what you say, but how you say it", though there are some word choices or "whats", that in feedback I would recommend you refrain from using, such as "you should", "you must", and "you need to". Your words can be weapons, or they can be used to affect one's interest in development.

> **In business today, the weapon of choice is often information and the way in which it is withheld or relayed.**

Be prepared to level with the employee, the follower of your leadership. It is not at all uncommon for leaders to be afraid of hurting the feelings of an employee who is typically a good performer. The dilemma is that you will hurt the employee's feelings more, and lose his or her respect for you as a leader, if you don't shoot straight[31], and provide honest feedback. A leader needs simply to state what he or she wants from the employee, listen to the employee's response, acknowledge the emotions or feelings expressed, and then seek agreement and commitment to the goals and expectations. The purpose of this procedure is to enable the employee to say to anyone, "I know what my job is in this situation."[32] It's been said splendidly. There are three things that successful people, meaning those who develop others, do differently from those not as successful:

- Make the right assumptions about people.

- Ask the right questions about people.

- Give the right assistance to people.

Previous chapters give you the tools to make assumptions through observations and talent-seeking. They also give you the tools to formulate your own questions. This is where you learn how to give the right assistance and then stand back, as those followers just might provide some feedback to you that you must also be prepared to hear.

Allowing for input, focusing on growth, and helping employees to think on their own, as we have discussed in previous chapters, will create a self-monitoring of their progress. But a leader must also give candid, honest, and timely feedback, to facilitate successful self-monitoring and growth. Many times, we, as employees and not just managers trying to be leaders, fail to see all that we ourselves do. Feedback is the mirror talking back to the onlooker. Both you and those you manage, and wish to be leading, have a mirror.

It is the Delivery That Delivers the Message

How often have you spent hours crafting the perfect message and the perfect combination of words, only to have the receiver of those words completely misinterpret your meaning? Communication is a powerful tool. Knowing how to use it is a powerful talent. In giving feedback, it is essential to pay attention to the three elements of communication that we each use every day: some combination of word choice, tone of voice, and body language. Remember the example percentages of how it is believed to work in many cases? Word choice counts for approximately eight per cent of the meaning of the message you provide. Tone of voice counts for approximately twenty-five per cent of the meaning of the message you provide, and body language accounts for the remaining sixty- four per cent. Yes, that means that the time spent on crafting the words just the way you want them affects less than ten per cent of the entire message you intend to convey to the listener. This is most often the case in face to face interactions but does have several exceptions in which those statistics would not be quite so specific nor so drastic in the impact each element has on the message.

The words "fine", "nothing", and "interesting" all have multiple meanings in the dictionary. It is not the word that changes when the meaning changes, but the tone. Try the words "Meet me later". Can you think of a way in which those words could be said that would imply a manager was upset with an employee and needed urgently to speak with him or her that afternoon? Now, can you think of a way that a woman in a bar could speak those same words to a potential date, holding the same body posture as the manager before, using a different tone of voice to produce a completely different meaning? I thought so. "Body language" is a misnomer

all in and of itself. Many times, I was accused of being defensive, closed, not interested, not listening, obstinate, and several other descriptions, simply because my arms were crossed in front of my body. The truth is having one's arms_crossed is quite possibly the most comfortable position I have found. I am continuously talking with my arms and hands, and just want to rest them for a while. Crossing them gives me a place to put them. Broaden the interpretations you carry around with you about certain body language cues.

When I talk about the body language of facial expressions, my favorite example is a friend of mine from Queens, New York. She worked with me, and continuously walked around with a very sour look on her face in the retail store in which we were to be friendly to and actually help customers, in Houston, Texas. Every time someone would ask her what was wrong, she would say "nothing." This is what she would say until about the fiftieth time someone asked her what was wrong. Then the eyes, the eyebrows, the mouth, AND the words changed. We finally all figured out that in New York, people walk the streets making no eye contact and with no facial expressions. We were all working together in Texas, where all people smile larger than life. She had merely become accustomed to having a neutral expression on her face, and because it was not a broad Texas smile we naively thought she was mad all the time.

Body language interpretation happens almost instantaneous- ly. What are the employees, to whom you are providing valuable feedback, interpreting about your delivery? Or are they even listen- ing if the first few words or signs you choose are indicators of dis- aster? "We have a problem and we need to talk," usually means "Oh, boy, here we go."

We Need to Talk

Want to set your feedback session up for success? Try to lead into the fact that you need to talk by saying something other than "We need to talk." This is not about manipulation, nor is it about saying something you do not really mean, it is simply about being honest. You may need to talk to the employee, but you what you really need to do is provide feedback. Perhaps you could say just that.

The age-old signals of battle about to be done are the words "We need to talk," or "Can you stop by my office on the way out?" or "There are a few things I need to tell you." While all of them are true, each phrase lacks a little piece of the story and can start a conflict even before you start the conversation. Those to whom you speak these words arrive in your office with invisible boxing gloves on, ready to do battle.

Feedback does not equal conflict, but it can be the spring- board to it, if not handled effectively. One way to handle it effectively is to think of *clarifying* an issue, as opposed to *confronting* an issue. If your intent is to confront someone and tell him or her that what they are doing is wrong, then you are barking up the tree of conflict. If, instead, what you are attempting to do is clarify the person's reasoning behind a certain behavior or response, then you are beginning what could be a successful feedback session.

What if Conflict Arises Instead of Feedback?

Certainly, it's not likely your intention to start a conflict, but if you do, or you feel you may end up there, it is best if you follow these ten principles before, during, and after.

Address all issues privately, not publicly

Most people would rather die by fire or drowning than speak in public. Because a public feedback session will mean that the employee will have to defend himself in public, the reaction you receive in a public confrontation will be very different from one in a private setting.

Address all issues as soon as possible.

This is more natural than dragging out the process both of what you will say and what the other person may have to anticipate in the way of your feedback.

Speak to one issue at a time.

If you overload the person with issues, both relevant and irrelevant, past, present, and future, you risk clouding the focus issue and damaging the person's self-esteem all at the same time. An attacked self-esteem can become defensive and irrational, making the interaction worse than it needs to be.

Make your point and then leave it alone.

No one likes a nag. Most adults understand what you say the first time, if they listen and if you say it in their language. Unless you truly perceive a lack of understanding, there is no need to continue to wield the news like a weapon. Express it, and then let them digest it and respond.

Address only issues the person can change.

If you ask a person to do something that he or she is completely incapable of doing, both of you are guaranteed frustration.

Avoid using humor that can be construed as sarcasm.

Your sense of humor may be fit for the comedy hour, but if the tone is too sarcastic, it may tell the person that you believe yourself to be above her or worse yet, her to be beneath you.

Avoid extreme language.

Words such as always, forever, and never are rarely accurate and frequently create unnecessary defensiveness when the receiver responds to the exaggeration.

Present feedback as questions, suggestions, recommendations or possible options for doing something differently.

This approach will allow the employee to think for himself as opposed to feeling as if he is being given no choice. Adults like to have choices and do not take kindly to dictatorial commands.

Avoid apologizing for the meeting.

Even if it arises out of conflict, your apology for it may indicate that you are not sure you were in the right to do what you did, say what you said, or address what you set out to address. You may acknowledge that you are sorry that they have certain feelings, if they express them to you, but it is your responsibility to share feedback in an appropriate manner and their responsibility to listen to it in an appropriate manner. Notice, I did not say accept it, but listen to it.

Use compliments sincerely and frequently.

The sandwich method really does work well, as long as it's used in a way that's sincere. Try sharing one compliment, then one constructive piece of feedback or suggestion, followed by another positive piece of information or compliment. When sandwiched between two compliments, difficult feedback is much easier to swallow.[33]

Ten Listening Guidelines for Leaders:

1. Address all issues privately, not publicly

2. Address all issues as soon as possible

3. Speak to one issue at a time

4. Make your point and then leave it alone

5. Address only issues the person can change

6. Avoid using humor than can be construed as sarcasm

7. Avoid extreme language

8. Present feedback as questions, suggestions, recommendations or possible options for doing something differently

9. Avoid apologizing for the meeting

10. Use compliments sincerely and frequently

Hunger is uncomfortable; famine is deadly

The most successful businessmen and women, managers, politicians, religious figure-heads, public speakers, and leaders who work with people, know one simple fact: Every person in the world is hungry. Yes, every person in this world is in fact hungry for something, and this type of appetite is not like craving salt or a chocolate bar. It is a craving for recognition, companionship, understanding, approval, and on and on and on.[34]

One of the things I have seen and read about repeatedly is everyone's need to feel worthwhile. This varies only in outward demonstration and request for such feedback, generationally, so be not easily fooled. Just because a younger person in your office *appears* to act entitled, he or she is still in need of feeling worthwhile. People want to feel important. Mary Kay Ash knew it. The teacher of Helen Keller knew it. Jack Canfield and Mark Victor Hansen knew it. All of the teachers of self-esteem and motivation know it and thrive on it. And leaders know it and do something about it. If you can develop your feedback skills to make others feel important and worthwhile, I would argue there is no higher compliment you could pay them and no higher compliment you'll get in return than loyal and continuous engaged interest and performance.

Utilize feedback to help that person feel useful by guiding him in the right direction. Help her find satisfaction by showing her progress toward a clearly stated goal. Help him experience significance by allowing for options, customization, or modification of your feedback. Yours is not the only way (we have had this discussion), but it can spark someone's sense of creativity to come up with some new conclusion that he may then share with you.

Sharing feedback will feed the hunger, but just like eating, it must be done consistently in order to promote healthy responses to the nourishment. If you withhold regular feedback, you are likely to find yourself in a position of suddenly having to administer extra-special efforts so that the nourishment will be taken. I have watched a patient take the slow road from surgery, taking intravenous nourishment for two or three days, to trying to stomach soft foods like applesauce, soup, and pudding. Once this hurdle is crossed, the transition from applesauce to apples is a bit more difficult. It can sometimes take four or five days for someone who has been starved of what we consider normal nourishment to become accustomed to and accepting of the real stuff. Think of how long those employees have gone without a regular dose of feedback. Are you feeding a hunger or a famine? You may have to take one small step at a time instead of handing them a fully loaded fries and a hamburger.

Just do it!

It was a brilliant marketing campaign for Nike, but "just doing it" is also what you are left with when you analyze the situation and take into consideration the obstacles and possible consequences when in the business of developing people. So, when it comes to feedback, what are you waiting for? For that matter, when it comes to anything worth doing, what the heck are you waiting for? The world is full of waiters, and they do not all work in food or drink establishments. Record books, halls of fame, banks and museums are full of doers.

The way you "do" feedback is to follow a simple model and avoid conflict. One model that I have found particularly helpful is the feedback meeting. Obviously, this type of meeting is more formal, yet in some cases this is good prototype to use to set the standard for future feedback encounters. It is also effective to use in situations where you feel the feedback may be construed as damaging or incite conflict. To achieve the greatest success, this meeting must be well planned. The first step is to form the purposes of the specific meet-ing you plan to have. Generally, the purposes of a feedback meet- ing include some or all of the following:

- To review the results and form conclusions from them

- To determine opportunities for actions to be taken

- To form an agreement (or contract) about what to do next[35]

It is also important to determine what type of communication style you will be using, based on the person to whom you are giving feedback. If you are a bottom line person but your recipient is more detailed oriented, you may want to adjust your style to reflect more details, if you wish the message to get through. Best practice suggests that you consider who you are talking to, the impact the meeting will have, questions that may arise, and the desired end result. If you don't look at these considerations, you are randomly aiming for a target that you cannot see. I do not recommend that approach.

I have also used much less formal approaches such as water cooler conversations, conference calls, and impromptu "touch base" calls. Asking for feedback regularly afforded me the opportunity to simply ask, "Any questions, comments, thoughts, or feed- back?" on a team conference call. This request alone gained me a lot of information and gave me the perfect opening to share team feedback.

For one-on-one, less formal feedback sessions, I would simply pick up the phone and begin asking questions. "Were you aware of how that sounded?" "Were you aware of what impact your actions had?" Most of the time, the employee was expecting my call if they felt they had made an error. Almost always, when I began with a question, the employee saw the implications and came up with a better plan for next time. It is amazing what one can accomplish by asking and listening, instead of telling and barking. Would that be a solution that might work for you? (Notice the lack of a woof?)

But, I Wanna Be the Favorite on the Playground!

Being a leader affords you a great many benefits, gifts, and good experience. It may even in some cases give you the big- headed feeling of being liked by all, if done effectively. Leaders develop and guide and coach and mentor. They do not make promises just to make people happy, or give only feedback that people want to hear, for the sake of being well liked. If your fear in giving feedback is that the employee will not like you anymore, then take your sand shovel and bucket and go back to the beginner sandbox. This is not about being the favorite playmate; it is about developing people into the best that they can be.

There will be times when you must deliver feedback that the employee will not want to hear, will not like to hear. Well, my goodness. Whom do you respect more, those who tell you the truth, even if it hurts, or those who make you temporarily feel good with a fib or an outright lie? If you hesitated, really give that some thought. Your job as a manager is to monitor and manage performance. Your job as a leader is to develop the people who first followed you because of your character and are now willing to follow your leadership because of what you stand for and who you are. Not liking what they hear, is often not the same as not liking who it came from, though if you are sensitive about this issue, the two will often appear very similar.

With those I have managed, I have found on many occasions the need to separate friendship from a professional working relationship. This is a skill and one that can be tested during times of tough feedback. One beautiful thing that usually came out of being able to separate these relationships effectively was that I was able to give feedback and then sit back and get some appropriate feed- back on how I delivered the message (or for that matter how I was doing just about anything).

If you have followed the lessons of leadership in this book and shoot straight with those who choose to follow you, you may find that they become long-time friends or at least good acquaintances. Your friends provide feedback naturally, so be careful what you dish out, as you are surely likely to get some in return.

Wait Just One Cotton-Pickin' Minute!

Me: "What do you mean, you think I could have done that better? That was not really the point of this entire conversation or the meeting here in my office."

Employee: "Yes, but you have always encouraged me to speak my opinion and share with you what I thought, and I just thought you could have handled that differently."

Me: "Er, uh, okay, you have a point. Touché. What are your thoughts about how you would have done this differently?"

That was a painful experience, the first time I had an employ- ee take my words, turn them around, and fire them back at me. How do you argue with a good point that you have already made yourself when it is made back at you? I quickly figured out that if I was going to be willing to dish it, then I had better also be willing to take it. After all, I am not perfect, and all along I have encouraged those that worked with me to be aware that in some ways they know more about things than I do. Fortunately, the "What have I done?!" feeling only lasted for a moment.

Feedback Guidelines:
(for you, your boss, and those you have the privilege of leading)

1. Define Appropriate

2. Define Timing: Set aside specific times when feedback on your actions is accepted openly, perhaps a day after or in private, depending on the situation.

3. Define Respectful Behavior: Create a system or signal that indicates times in which feedback would not be taken well and needs to be deferred.

4. Clarify Facts vs. Emotions: Describe the need for fact-based information and non-emotional outbursts.

5. Define Professionalism: Describe the need for the degree of professionalism; subject to your needs and personal definition of this term.

Obviously, feedback to the leader or the manager or the boss requires different tactics based on your comfort level, your company culture, and the severity of the situation. Either way, I encourage you to allow for it and decide how it is best delivered. The same methods I have suggested can be used for sharing with those you lead and manage for their purposes, or for those who lead and manage you, so that you can share appropriate feedback with them. Keep in mind that what you do as a leader is not always automatically what those who lead or manage you will subscribe to, believe in, or proactively embrace. For that matter, after reading this book, you may find yourself teaching those who manage you how to do it differently.

Tread lightly and have a plan. You do have a plan, don't you?

*Keep reading. I've provided one for you,
just in case we needed it...*

10 LEADERS CONTINUE TO IMPROVE

Were this a training class, I would now toss a ball (a soft one, don't worry!) at each of you and ask you to verbalize one thing you have learned so far. However, this is not a class, nor a drill, but real life, and this is the point at which you get to make a choice. What do you do now? Put the book down and pat yourself on the back for reading it? Given book reading stats of late, that is not a bad option. Do you look at a few things from a new vantage point and promise to put a few items on your already crowded "to-do" list, or task bar, or task keeping app? Or, do you manage to become a leader? Do you begin to implement, if you have not already? The universe does not reward you for reading; the universe, teams, boss, and companies do reward actions.

What are you willing to do to become the leader you want to be? If you have read all the way through nine chapters to get here, congratulations! If not, I was raised to tell you to get to the back of the line, or in this case, the front of the book, but who are we kidding? With attention spans at an all-time low, everyone bragging about how darned busy they are, and more tasks vying for our attention than we ever imagined, maybe this is the best you can do, so go for it. You will need the knowledge from the preceding chapters to apply here, but as in all new skills, you'll need time to practice and can pick up additional skills as you continue to progress or even to work backwards. Just remember to remain disciplined. You and the team you lead, deserve your effort.

Your progress plan and efforts to take action will be an ongoing process that benefits from practice. Nothing in this book is a magic bullet, though there are some techniques that you can implement immediately. Some are easier than others; many require a shift in thinking, which may have already happened. Take two items at a time that you want to change and master those before choosing to work on two more. Just a few days of repetition will help to form the basis of a habit and behavioral change, but keep in mind that mastery of any new skill is a continuing effort. Congrats for getting started and let's get started!

> **Take two items at a time that you wish to change and master those before choosing to work on two more.**

Progress Plan Phase 1: Get Ready!

Give each chapter a quick skim through. Yes, that means go back and look at the notes you made, scan those gray boxes a second time and simply refresh your mind on what you have read. For a quick refresh, in CHAPTER 1, we looked at each person's uniqueness and the fact that he or she does not, in fact, work for the sheer pleasure of seeing your smiling face each and every day, though we speak as if each employee works expressly FOR us or the company in which both the leader and employee work. We examined the effect that this type of verbiage, the questions we ask, and other subtleties o our actions and words have on those we lead, before, during, and after times of change. And, most importantly, interwoven in the conversation of respect and value, we began to open the real conversation about emotional intelligence and how to use it. In fact, we even introduced an abbreviated quiz (CORE Snapshot™) and its larger full profile (CORE MAP®), that does more than label. Here is the quiz link again: www.ContagiousCompanies.com/CORESnapshot.

In CHAPTER 2, we then looked closely at the impact of focusing on an employee's growth as a high priority. The advantages we discovered are increased loyalty and a sense of achievement. We paid special attention to recognizing an employee's or follower's strengths AND weaknesses and, based on those, learned how to set clear expectations and lead a person to achievement of both professional and personal goals. Of course, we also had to decide at what point one cares or does not care about the personal growth of an employee.

CHAPTER 3 brought us into the domain of asking for help, previously perceived as an absolute "no-no" for this once self-confessed control freak. Asking for help was said to bring others into the loop, make reasonable standards actually achievable, and gain buy-in, engagement, and support from those you have the privilege of leading. The primary caution here was to choose wisely whom you ask, when you ask, and what promises you make about what you'll do with their counsel. As with anything else, think before you speak, or in this case, ask.

What we discovered in CHAPTER 4 was that letting go is tougher than we thought. The virtues of micro-management were quickly dismissed, except in certain special circumstances. What we found is that new employees often need close supervision the most, and that veteran employees who have not yet proven their ability to survive without it, may be subject to some heavy performance documentation and managing-out of the organization options. Above all, we stressed that if you micro-managed inappropriately, but had built open communication and expressed good intentions, you would probably be forgiven, as long as you backed off when the employee asked you or let you know it was encroaching on his or her performance.

Thus CHAPTER 5 appropriately focused forgiving the mistakes of others, knowing that we ourselves would make a few along the way. Forgiving others' mistakes took a different twist, however, when we mentioned the need to do so even when the committer of the crime did not apologize. Eek! We looked at the need for complete clarity and how everything is subject to interpretation. Then we tried to resolve the issue of how many mistakes is too many and where you draw the line. It is different for each of you, like your need for recognition.

Each of the employees you manage will benefit from what you learned in CHAPTER 6, as each of them will find new feelings of value if you give them the recognition that is needed. Of course, one of the keys to this chapter is realizing that each person's needs are different, and it is important to ask people how *they* would like to be recognized. There are many means of low-cost, low-fat, free, and fun recognition out there and some were listed, as were the best ways to determine the level of recognition needs in your organization or workplace. This will benefit you, them, and everyone you work with, almost as much as clear communication.

If you followed all of the meat and potatoes in CHAPTER 7, you learned the importance of one of the single most taken-for- granted skills on the planet, is communication. We discussed the fact that it is a two-way street and fraught with opportunities for error. We also examined the critical role listening plays in this process, as much of the chapter is on listening skills and the importance of them. Huh? Just checking. Isn't that what many of the fine folk you lead are saying when you use buzzwords or highly technical language or speak in a communication style that differs greatly from their own?

We also worked on those things that differ in CHAPTER 8, didn't we? We touched mainly on opinions here, as opposed to communication styles, but the concept would apply to all things and merely refocused our efforts on valuing the ideas, concepts, opinions and needs of others, even if they are different from our own. We talked of additional ways to value others, show respect, spark creativity, and ignite productive behavior and input solicitation.

What we did not cover was left for CHAPTER 9 when we dis- cussed the important element of giving honest feedback and learn- ing to take what you dish out. That was a toughie, but by and large, we covered the difference between constructive criticism and feedback, as well as the delivery dynamics that mold a message. We focused on the hunger each person has to feel special, and we also gave ways, ten of them, to avoid a poorly done feedback session that erupts into conflict. We then offered a caution about the need to be liked by all.

Don't believe for one minute that the exercises you are about to undertake here in Chapter 10 will cause, make, force, or even entice everyone out there in the playground of life to like you or make them easy to lead. It is a nice pipe dream and one that I wish I could sell you, but I am afraid you would be standing in a long line of folks also wanting to buy a bridge over water in the desert. People may be jealous of your new-found skills; they may find reason to scoff at your efforts to change; they may even tell you that what you have read and want to try, will not work; and you know what? If you don't believe it will, it won't. Either way, you get to be right, but I thought you wanted to be successful. Avoid focusing on the reactions of others and the possible effort it may take you to change some habits that have been with you a while, and focus on where you're going and how quickly you'd like to arrive. Besides, it is not uncommon in the early stages of a new promotion, for those who were not promoted, to purposely make it appear as if you were the wrong choice. You weren't and with these steps you can make a difference and become a better leader without all the hassles and headaches of attempting to learn it the hard way. You with me?

Here the first bit of clarity to gather. Decide what you want to work on from each chapter and write down each new behavior or way of thinking you desire. Write the question and your answer in a notebook or journal. Here are your guiding questions and space to write if you happen to be reading this book on good old-fashioned paper.

Steps for Progress Plan Phase 1: Get Ready

1. Review Each Chapter

2. Record Each Chapter Action Item from Phase 1 Questions

3. See Yourself Achieving the Changes

4. Practice and Keep Going!

Step 1: What is one thing I will do to reinforce the concept that Employees Are Unique People, and that Leaders Respect and Value Their Uniqueness?

Step 2: What is one thing I will do to show that I am Interested in Their Growth, Almost As Much As They Are?

Step 3: What is one thing I will do to Ask Help from Those I Lead, as They Are Closer To The Problem Than I am?

Step 4: What is one thing I will do to Micro-Manage Only Those Who Need It, And Only Until They Prove They Don't Need It?

Step 5: What is one thing I will do to demonstrate that I Allow and Forgive Their Mistakes, Even If They Don't Apologize?

Step 6: What is one thing I will do to indicate my understanding that Praise is Powerful and a Priority, If They Need It, and to Find Out If They Do?

Step 7: What is one thing I will do to Speak to Them Clearly, and Give New Meaning To Talk the Talk, while then stopping to Listen Up?

Step 8: What is one thing I will do to Allow For my Own Opinions and For Theirs, Even If They Are Dissimilar or Vastly Different?

Step 9: What is one thing I will do in order to facilitate Giving Them Honest Feedback and Learning To Take What I Dish Out?

Bonus question: What tool will I use, or method will I engage to better understand just how those I lead are different with reference to their personalities and how I might modify them differently based on using emotional intelligence(EQ)?

Stop for a moment now that you've read, or possibly even answered all of the questions. Visualize exactly how things would look if you were to make these changes. Your brain will not sabotage you in this way. If you can imagine things being better, your leadership being not just good, but great, then you have the ability and competence to do so. All that is left is putting forth the effort and maybe the practice

Phase One is complete when you have a list of items to accomplish that you can actually see yourself doing. If you now have more than ten items on your list, choose your ten highest priorities and use these for Phase Two. You must first lead yourself to your high priorities before you can lead others to anything.

> **You must first lead yourself to focus on your highest priorities before you can lead others to anything.**

Progress Plan Phase Two: Get set!

Once you have compiled your list of NO MORE THAN TEN ITEMS, record them in your journal or below if you have a hard copy book.

To become a leader, I will:

1.

2.

3.

4.

5.

6.

7.

8.

9.

10.

Part of programming the subconscious to work on achieving these items for you, even when you are not thinking about them, is achieved in the exercise of writing and rewriting them. Should you choose not to write your items down, you are sabotaging your efforts, as the items you keep in your head are only ideas; the items you write down are much more likely to become actions, and the universe rewards actions. Sound familiar? If you want to begin referring to teammates as employees who work with you instead of employees who work for you, but you never write that desire down or do anything about it, then the want is just an idea and has little or no value, at least in this culture. Think about that.

However, even after you write them all down, you will overload yourself if you attempt all ten actions at one time. Thus, there is a need to see which ones warrant your immediate attention and which ones can be sidelined momentarily. Take each one of your items and rate, on the next page, the impact that each is having on your ability to lead others. The rating scale will reflect the amount of leadership this item is costing you. A rating of five would mean that if you do not implement this action item, you will be hampering yourself greatly. Fives keep you in management instead of leadership. A rating of one would indicate that this item is a small challenge, costing you a little leadership, but that there are other problems to look at first.

> **How badly you want something is not solely reflected in the amount of effort you put forth to attain it, but also in the amount of planning, preparing, diligence and follow through you extend to make sure it happens.**

Circle the rating that most closely matches the cost (5 being highest, 1 being lowest) of not following through on the action item you have listed.

Leadership Cost Matrix
How much leadership would no change cost you?

Action Items   Cost of No Change

1. _____   1   2   3   4   5
2. _____   1   2   3   4   5
3. _____   1   2   3   4   5
4. _____   1   2   3   4   5
5. _____   1   2   3   4   5
6. _____   1   2   3   4   5
7. _____   1   2   3   4   5
8. _____   1   2   3   4   5
9. _____   1   2   3   4   5
10. _____   1   2   3   4   5

Now, on your paper or in your book, draw a vertical line in the space between the 3's and the 4's, from the top to the bottom of the matrix. Any circles to the right of the line are danger signs. These action items are your highest priorities right now that deserve your specific and ardent focus.

Had I completed this assessment when I first began to manage at the ripe old age of eighteen, I would have recorded "Ask for input from employees" as an immediate action item. I would then have marked it a "five" cost, as not asking for input caused me to repeatedly make decisions in isolation and suffer the consequences. There was no buy-in from the team and certainly no ownership from the employees of the grand decisions I was making. As there was no involvement, there was no commitment, and consequently many of my grand ideas and plans failed miserably. If I had chosen not to begin asking for input, I would have continued a practice that was holding me back from being a leader, instead of merely a manager.

When one crosses the line, one is in big trouble. Observe those items that fall to the right of your line, those that you rated either a four or a five in cost. Those are the items that deserve your immediate attention and for which we will create an action plan and picture of success. Be sure to create your action plan for these items as specifically a possible, to avoid the trap of the shotgun and snake approach.

The Shot Gun and the Snake Approach

A man went fishing in a swamp and upon passing under trees watched a snake fall from a tree into his boat. Responding quickly and in fear, he grabbed his gun and shot at the snake. He missed the snake but managed to hit his boat and create a hole in the bottom.

Morale of the story: Don't use the shotgun approach to your problems, or you may find yourself sunk.

If all ten of your action items fall on the right of the line, don't lose heart. You now know what issues to work on. I recommend you work on the top two first, the top three five-rated items next and then the rest if they are still an issue. The top, next, and following most important items are, of course, subject to your discretion and to what all improvements or changes occur when you begin to consciously focus on your own leadership development.

If none of your items fall to the right of the line, merely choose to work on those which rated the highest, and work back- ward in numerical order from there.

At the most, work on only three of your action items at a time in order to allow yourself the ability to truly focus on change. The law of diminishing returns will take effect if you try to work on all, or even five, of them at a time. Your efforts will be strong at first, then you will see slip-ups, then you will begin to slack off in your efforts, and then you will simply stop working on them. One does not learn to play football by learning all the defensive plays, equipment needed, teams in the league, and attending three practices all in one day. One learns by tackling one item at a time, sometimes literally.

Steps for Progress Plan Phase 2: Get Set!

1. List your ten, or less, action items

2. Rate each item in the Leadership Cost Matrix

3. Denote which items "cross the line"

4. Decide which items are the top two most important

5. Get set to see some rapid progress!

Progress Plan Phase Three: Go!

You now have a list of several items that need your attention. If you do nothing, your situation will not simply continue, but quite possibly become worse, or even become the norm. Detrimental things left unaddressed often become the normal way of doing things.

Before you tackle any of your action items, no matter how much they are costing you, it will be important for you to decide how things need to be different. If you struggle with giving feed- back and shy away from it, every time, fearing conflict and confrontation more than most fear the dentist, then decide what your next encounter should look like instead. To simply say, "I will begin to deliver feedback openly and honestly," if you have not defined what that would look like for you, that action item alone will not necessarily point you in the direction of success you're seeking.

For each of your action items, answer the following questions and begin to transform your ideas and desires into mental pictures. These questions will begin to create your *Transformaction Plan*™.

- What behaviors are you using now that you wish to change?

- What is your short-term goal?

- What does the result specifically look like for you when you achieve your goal?

- When will you achieve this transformation?

Though it may appear tedious, answer each of these four questions for each one of your two action items you have chosen to work on first. Keep in mind the guideline for goal-setting that we discussed in earlier chapters. It's tried and true, older than me and than you, and still works as a simple guideline. Keep goals SMART. In your answers that describe the how, when, and what of your goals, you must ensure that your goals and desires are:

S — Specific

M — Measurable

A — Attainable

R — Recorded

T — Timed

Review each of your eight answers, and if you do not have eight, go back to answering questions until you do. (Eight answers are derived from four questions for two action items). In your review, you are ensuring that you have recorded measurable time- lines, as well as specific and attainable visions of what your new behaviors and actions will be once you achieve success or master this new skill.

Obviously goals present obstacles, but they also have benefits. Goals, including each of your action items, have smaller steps that can be achieved that are a part of the larger achievement. None of what you are working on will necessarily be easy and achieved with the snap of your managerial, soon to be leadership, fingers. Taking our analysis one step further, and articulating those obstacles, benefits, and smaller steps, will go a long way toward that finger snapping action, though you still have to follow the steps you record. For each action item you have chosen and using the answers to the four *Transformaction Plan*™ questions, then complete a *Goal Template*™ or recreate the template information on a spreadsheet or in your journal.

By clearly articulating the desired benefits, you tell yourself why you are working to achieve what you have said is an important goal. These benefits will help you when you encounter an obstacle, and you will. The articulation of each step will give you things that you can do right here, right now, and thus feel the sense of achievement of having done *something*, even if a little thing toward the achievement of your goal.

```
+-----------------------------------------------------------------+
|                     GOAL TEMPLATE ®                              |
+-----------------------------------------------------------------+
| GOAL:                        | ACTIVITIES TO ACHIEVE GOAL        |
| • _____  |      (IN PRIORITY ORDER)          |
|   _____  | STEP ONE:                         |
|   _____  |                                   |
|   _____  |   _____    |
|                              |   _____    |
|   +-----------------------+  |   _____    |
|   | TIMELINE: _____ |  |   _____    |
|   |  _____  |  |   _____    |
| BENEFITS:                    | STEP TWO:                         |
| • _____  |                                   |
|   _____  |   _____    |
|   _____  |   _____    |
|   _____  |                                   |
|                              |                                   |
| OBSTACLES:                   | STEP THREE:                       |
| • _____  |   _____    |
| • _____  |   _____    |
| • _____  |   _____    |
| • _____  | STEP FOUR:                        |
|                              |   _____    |
| ADDITIONAL KNOWLEDGE:        |   _____    |
| PEOPLE TO CONTACT:           |   _____    |
| • _____  | STEPS FIVE – ACHIEVEMENT:         |
| • _____  |   _____    |
| • _____  |   _____    |
| • _____  |   _____    |
| • _____  |   _____    |
|                              |   _____    |
| AFFILIATIONS NEEDED:         |   _____    |
| • _____  |   _____    |
| • _____  |   _____    |
| • _____  |   _____    |
| • _____  |   _____    |
| • _____  |   _____    |
| • _____  |   _____    |
+-----------------------------------------------------------------+
|        P.O. Box 683316  Orlando, FL 32868-3316                  |
|     Toll Free: 1-866-382-0121  Fax: 407-877-8366                |
| contagiouscompanies.com   Monica@contagiouscompanies.com        |
+-----------------------------------------------------------------+
```

Once you have completed *Goal Templates*® for each of your first two action items, you will want to post them in a place where you can see them. Whether others see them or not is up to you, but I would not recommend it, as others tend to be less than supportive of our efforts to make changes, particularly if they will be negatively affected by the changes or have never been able to make changes themselves. I have carried my goal templates in my portfolio or planner or on a file in my phone, for years. I see them three or four times a day, on purpose or by accident when I'm looking for something.

You are the driving force behind all that you achieve. Mastery of your first few goals and action items will be up to you. Progress made after that will be up to you. Goals change and will be modified subject to your approval and yours alone. If you feel you have mastered your goal number one, then pick the next one from your list, so that you are always working on both or looking ahead at the next one. A body in motion stays in motion. Stop focusing on improvement and the temptation to become sedentary and "just the way I'm wired" can become tempting and render you habitually ineffective, and possibly make you miss opportunities. Each effort may take a different amount of time and action. Each one may appear easy at first and then get harder. Each one may appear again after you thought you had mastered it. Old habits die hard. Go at it again, as you will find many of your skills and behaviors do not possess a beginning and end point but are always works in progress.

Once you have determined what you want to work on, what you want it to look like, when you want it, and what stands in your way of reaping all of the benefits you will have once you follow the steps to get there… it is up to you.

Steps for Progress Plan Phase 3: GO!

1. Choose three action items to work on first.

2. Answer Transformaction Plan™ questions for each.

3. Follow SMART goal guidelines.

4. Complete a Goal Template™ for each of the three action items.

5. Add an action item, as one is completed, until all are completed

Get ready, get set, GO!

FINAL THOUGHTS

O ne of the greatest barriers to people becoming who they want to be is fear of failure, or in some cases fear of success, particularly if you've not had much of it. One of the greatest barriers to becoming a better leader is believing you have to fake it or be someone else to be successful. That's based on rejection of who you really are and fear of failure in an attempt to connect with others. No matter how we want to develop leadership skills, that concept is a foundational principle and I have seen time and time again just how much your ability to become a better leader is based first on emotional intelligence and then on the skills you choose to develop.

If you fear failing, invite the option in and learn to live with it, while focusing on clearly seeing how much better things will be should you muster the effort and manage to change them. The same is true for fear of success and another popular barrier which is over planning in the pursuit of perfection. People are not perfect, but we've said that already. People are, no matter your personality, age, gender, background, choices, actions, past, present or parents, ALL able to be and become and even become better, leaders.

You've come this far, even brought your fears with you. What are you waiting for? What is keeping you from being able to catch on, catch up, or simply pursue becoming a *Contagious Leader*? No one will give you what you want to be easily, and leadership is not an accomplishment achieved nor earned while on auto pilot. Only you can be who you want to be and put forth the effort to make and take on opportunities that align with your goals and desires. If you are manager, a parent, a friend, a janitor, a cook, an entrepreneur, a photographer, a motivational speaker, a gardener, a stay-at-home mom, a stay- at-home dad, a real-estate broker, a rocket-scientist, a window- washer, a computer engineer, a sanitation engineer, a grocery bagger, a banker, social media marketer, or anything else...

You can manage to become a leader...

And your influence will be CONTAGIOUS!

ACKNOWLEDGMENTS

It is true that no book happens by magic or osmosis or miraculous intervention. People make the miracle happen, and quite a few people have been instrumental in the little miracle of the book you now hold in your hand.

My sincere gratitude goes to Lynne Barga and Nat Wofford, my parents, for giving me the base of knowledge that provided the foundation for what you read here. Vera and Bill Barga provided an additional layer and Kay and David Edmondson continued to add to what I knew and learned. Close friends who provided wisdom and encouragement, as well as support, include Chris Lubniewski, Dr. Joseph Juliano, Lisa Wayne, Max Narro, Darren Lacroix, Bob Biferie, and Tracy Ross. My special thanks and undying appreciation go to Lee Harrelson for helping me find the courage to go out on my own, and who believed in me more than I believed in myself.

The company in which I grew up as a manager and developed into a leader was Cingular Wireless. Many thanks go to the colleagues who continually supported my sometimes unpopular ideas, encouraged my spirit, guided my drive, pushed when I felt like stopping, and questioned when I did not want to explain what I considered to be well known "truths". These colleagues include Royal Mowery, John Robertson, Doris Lake, Charles Jackson, Rich Guidotti, Dan Jones, Kathy Gray and Rob Lauber. The team that helped me to launch my dream into a reality, and helped make me the leader that I am today, includes Andrea Pickering, Cat Shea, Catherine Simmons, Debbie Lewellen, Eileen Rodriguez, James Malandro, Janet Hamilton, Linda Schexnaydre, Mark Draizin, Nydia Velez, Patty Moore, Sari Vicchini, Thad Merritt, Tracy Maddox, Dennis Lashbrook, Jamie Cornelius, Becky Busby, Larry Pate, and Keith Boteler. I could not have done it without each and every one of you!

Even more instrumental in the logistics of book creation are editors and designers extraordinaire. What you see is what they make look so easy! I also must thank the best book shepherd on the planet, Mr. Greg Godek, who managed to steer me in all the right directions, despite card-carrying control-freak resistance from the author. My thanks to each of them for their expertise, belief, and efforts.

END NOTES

Chapter 1

[1] Webster's New World Dictionary. Third College Edition. Editor: Victoria Neufeldt. New York: Webster's New World. 1988.

[2] Covey, Steven. _7 Habits of Highly Effective People_. Simon and Schuster: New York. 1989. p101

[3] Pacetta, Frank. _Don't Fire Them, Fire Them Up: Motivate Yourself and Your Team_. New York: Simon and Shuster. 1994. p 212.

[4] Fournies, Ferdinand. _Coaching for Improved work Performance_. New York: Liberty-hall Press. 1978. p42-43

[5] How to Deliver Exceptional Customer Service, Seminar Workbook; Fred Pryor Seminars.p 14.

[6] Mackay, Harvey. _Beware the Naked Man who offers you his shirt_. New York: Fawcett Columbine. 1990.

[7] Fournies, Ferdinand. _Coaching for Improved work Performance_. New York: Liberty-hall Press. 1978. p42-43

[8] Alessandra, Tony. _New Edition: Relationship Strategies_. Illinois: Nightingale Conant.

Chapter 2

[9] Buckingham, Marcus; Coffman, Curt; *First Break All the Rules New York*: Simon and Schuster. 1999.

[10] Buckingham, Marcus; Coffman, Curt; *First Break All the Rules New York*: Simon and Schuster. 1999.

[11] author unknown

[12] http://www.marykay.com/; Mary Kay Ash 1/2003

Chapter 4

[13] Bergmann, Hurson, Russ-Eft. *Everyone a Leader: A Grassroots Model for the New Workplace*. Achieve Global. New York: John Wiley & Sons, Inc. 1999. pg 65

[14] *Entrepreneur* magazine August 2003, page 10 Rieva Lesonsky Editor's Note

[15] Business Psychology News, Vol 99.1 on internet http://www. businesspsychologosit.come/bpnews201.html 5/23/03

Chapter 5

[16] Bridges, William. *Managing Transitions* . p 44

[17] Buckingham, Marcus; Coffman, Curt; *First Break All the Rules New York*: Simon and Schuster. 1999. p117.

Chapter 6

[18] Nelson, Bob. *1001 Ways to Reward Employees*, New York: Workman Publishing. 1994. pgs:xi

[19] Bergmann, Hurson, Russ-Eft. *Everyone a Leader: A Grassroots Model for the New Workplace*. Achieve Global. New York: John

Wiley&Sons, Inc. 1999. pg 165

[20] Nelson, Bob. *1001 Ways to Reward Employees*. New York: Workman Publishing. 1994. pgs10-15

[21] Nelson, Bob. *1001 Ways to Reward Employees*. New York: Workman Publishing. 1994. pgs10-15

[22] Canfield, Jack. *Self-Esteem and Peak Performance*. Boulder: CareerTrack.

Chapter 7

[23] John R. Schermerhorn, Jr., James G. Hunt, Richard N. Osborn. *Organizational Behavior*, 7th Edition (2002), pp190-191.

[24] Allen C. Bluedorn, Carol Felker Kaufman, and Paul M. Lane, "How Many Things Do You Like to Do at Once?" Academy of Management Executive, Vol. 6 (November 1992), pp. 17-26.

[25] John R. Schermerhorn, Jr., James G. Hunt, Richard N. Osborn. *Organizational Behavior*, 7th Edition (2002), pp190-191.

[26] Covey, Steven. *7 Habits of Highly Effective People*. New York: Simon and Schuster. 1989, pp237-238

[27] Precker, Michael. BossWord Bingo. Dallas Morning News (Sept 17, 2002) p 1C

Chapter 8

[28] Eppler, Mark. *Management Mess-Ups*. New Jersey: Career Press. 1997, p36

[29] Gurney, Darrel W. "That'll Cost you Extra". Sharing Ideas. December-January 2001. p11

[30] Covey, Steven. *7 Habits of Highly Effective People*. Simon and Schuster: New York. 1989, p143

Chapter 9

[31] Stowell, Steven J., Starcevich, Mark M. *The Coach: Creating Partnerships for a Competitive Edge*. Oklahoma: The Center for Management and Organization Effectiveness. 1998, p105.

[32] Stowell, Steven J., Starcevich, Mark M. *The Coach: Creating Partnerships for a Competitive Edge*. Oklahoma: The Center for Management and Organization Effectiveness. 1998, p105.

[33] Maxwell, John C. *Developing the Leader Within You*. Nashville: Thomas Nelson publishers. 1993. p124.

[34] Maxwell, John C. *Developing the Leader Within You*. Nashville: Thomas Nelson. 1993. p116.

[35] Robinson, Dana Gaines, James C. Robinson. *Performance Consulting*. San Francisco: Barret-Koehler Publishers, 1996. pp257-258

CPSIA information can be obtained
at www.ICGtesting.com
Printed in the USA
LVHW04s1953031018
592296LV00005B/23/P